SWIMMING SYDNEY

CHRIS BAKER is a lifelong swimmer, educator and writer who was born and raised in Sydney. He has spent much of his professional life overseas, living and working in Vancouver, Prague, Hong Kong and Berlin. Chris was lured back to Sydney by its beautiful beaches, superb municipal pools, wild swimming holes and world-famous ocean baths. His favourite swimming venue in the world is Wylie's Baths in south Coogee.

'Part travel guide and part memoir, these
52 immersive essays – one a week – remind us how
inextricably Australian culture is linked to water and
our bodies. Immerse yourself and emerge invigorated,
like the best swims leave you feeling.'

BENJAMIN LAW

'Chris Baker takes a deep dive into the watery
history of Sydney, focusing by turns on its conflicted
history, ravishing beauty and salty present. His eye
for detail is sharper than a gull's, and while his love
of the liquid landscapes he traverses is palpable and
at times nostalgic, it is never sentimental. Reading
his 52 swims made me long to don my togs and to
get away from my own daily comfort pool. I ached
to rush to a dive-in, to slurp a Sunnyboy or chomp a
pluto pup, and above all, to immerse in the "dignified
consolation" that he offers in every chapter. This
book is both a keeper and a giver, an invitation and
a challenge, a guide and a gift; it's a love song to the
caress of watery wonder.'

AILSA PIPER

'A poetic ode to the water that will have you
reaching for your goggles and leaping into the blue.
Chris Baker may swim like a fish, but he also writes
like a dream. *Swimming Sydney* is a beguiling portrait
of love, loss, community and identity in
the world's most swimmable city.'

YVES REES

SWIMMING

SYDNEY

NEWSOUTH

UNSW Press acknowledges the Bedegal people, the Traditional Owners of the unceded territory on which the Randwick and Kensington campuses of UNSW are situated, and recognises the continuing connection to Country and culture. We pay our respects to Bedegal Elders past and present.

A NewSouth book

Published by
NewSouth Publishing
University of New South Wales Press Ltd
University of New South Wales
Sydney NSW 2052
AUSTRALIA
newsouthpublishing.com

© Chris Baker 2024
First published 2024

10 9 8 7 6 5 4 3 2 1

A catalogue record for this book is available from the National Library of Australia

ISBN: 9781761170270 (paperback)
         9781761179136 (ebook)
         9781761178238 (ePDF)

Design Josephine Pajor-Markus
Cover design Mika Tabata

Extract on page 24 from 'Five Bells' by Kenneth Slessor in *Selected Poems* (HarperCollins Publishers, 2014) reproduced with permission.

All reasonable efforts were taken to obtain permission to use copyright material reproduced in this book, but in some cases copyright could not be traced. The author welcomes information in this regard.

*To my brothers, who have swum with me
since I could dog paddle.*

*To the friends who swam with me and cheered me on –
Ray, Catherine, Sally, Charmaine, Toby and Marc.*

And to Wade, who keeps me buoyant.

Sydney's First Nations peoples have swum and played and fished in Sydney's precious waterways for thousands of years. Sovereignty of the lands and waters of Sydney was never ceded. I would like to acknowledge the Traditional Custodians of the land and waters of Sydney, and I pay my deep respects to their Elders past and present.

CONTENTS

WINTER

INTRODUCTION

One evening, when I was about ten years old, I watched a film on television called *The Swimmer*. Based on a short story by John Cheever, the film portrays a day in the life of Neddy Merrill, an athletic, middle-aged businessman who decides to 'swim' home via his neighbours' suburban pools.

To my prepubescent eyes, the film was wonderfully baffling. It featured a tanned and taut 53-year-old Burt Lancaster in the title role, sporting nothing but skimpy bathers and his extraordinary, oversized grin. As he progresses from pool to pool, Neddy encounters one martini-guzzling neighbour after another. He slaps a lot of backs, occasionally takes a sip from a highball himself, does a lap of a pool and then moves on.

The film resonated with me for many years. Its details, and indeed its general plot, were lost to me over time, but its mood and the image of Burt Lancaster 'swimming' home was forever chiselled into my memory. During my boyhood, I'd talk about *The Swimmer* with my brothers. Lolling on a pontoon moored in salt water, or dangling legs into a chlorinated backyard pool, we'd joke about what it would be like to jump fences in suburban Sydney and make our way home via its pools. How long a swim could we thread together? Which parts of the city would have the most pools, or the best pools, to follow? Later in life, when I spoke to friends my age who also liked to swim, I was surprised that the film had had a similar impact on them. Few of us had seen the movie recently, but we all agreed that it had lingered in our childhood consciousnesses as something strange and memorable.

Not long after I decided to write this book, I was able to see *The Swimmer* again. Serendipitously, it had been scheduled at the Art Gallery of New South Wales as part of a retrospective of films that were made in 1968. I was surprised and delighted to see a near-full auditorium for the Sunday afternoon screening, especially since it was a glorious early-autumn day that was not unlike the one that unfolds in the movie.

Within a few minutes of the movie's opening, I was awoken to the fact that it was a cinematic swimming myth. True to my fuzzy memories, Lancaster swims many a pool and gatecrashes the odd pool party. But, more poignantly, this strange film takes us on the odyssey of a man who is profoundly damaged and 'swimming' towards a personal reckoning. With each pool he traverses, his armour of nostalgia, privilege and delusion is gradually washed away, and he loses his emotional buoyancy. He and his booze-addled neighbours are representative of *Homo americanus*, white, rich and privileged in so many ways, yet utterly indifferent to the social and racial fault lines that are building in their country in the late 1960s.

Despite some dated psychedelic visual flourishes and an overwrought score by Marvin Hamlisch, *The Swimmer* played strongly to the contemporary audience, likely tapping into the politics of our times. Its white, middle-aged protagonist who represses unpleasant facts, and the strong women who call his bluff, seem to presage the Era of Trump and the #MeToo movement. More significantly, I think *The Swimmer*, like all myths, taps into something profound about the human condition and asks some remarkable questions. Can swimming be an initiation, a meditation, an expiation? Is swimming a metaphor for our individual navigation of life's emotional tides? Can a swim wash away the past and cleanse us emotionally?

Perhaps because I am now about the age that Burt Lancaster was when he swam his way through this film, these questions seem particularly pointed. Yet watching the movie made me think of boyhood as well as middle age, leading me to reflect on family, on friends, on struggles, on pleasures. It made me think of place as well as time, and of the many swims that I have done in Sydney. For me, swimming *is* Sydney. After a swim at one of Sydney's beaches or pools, I feel like I've had a mini holiday, renewed in spirit and reacquainted with the city's beauty and generosity. Swimming is the greatest joy of living in this city, and the one I have been most delighted to return to after living half my working life overseas. Whether shared or solo, my swims in Sydney are more than the pure motion of gliding through water. They speak of place, people and stories, and they give me a strong sense of belonging.

This book is a love letter to both the act of swimming and the city that boasts more aquatic pleasures than just about any other urban centre in the world. It is also a celebration of why we Sydneysiders take to the water, and of what it means to be buoyant in the many senses of the word. *Swimming Sydney* looks at how swimming and the healing element of water can help us to better understand ourselves, our city and our island nation.

The 52 swims of this book take place over the course of a calendar year. As I follow the seasons, I swim from Palm Beach to Cronulla, from Mount Druitt to Bondi. These chapters take us to iconic beaches, municipal pools, harbour enclosures, hidden rivers, tidal rock pools, bushland lakes and a backyard pool. They are also springboards for stories past and present, personal and universal. Some are enriched by First Nations' knowledge of Sydney's waterways, others muse on how swimming informs popular culture. They recount Olympic champions and surfing legends, extol the benefits of cold-water swimming for depression, evoke the submarine invasions of Sydney Harbour, and visit a site reputed for its apparitions of the Virgin Mary.

Taking my weekly plunges, I swim with the many tribes of Sydney: a septuagenarian aqua aerobics class; a six-month-old baby learning to swim; a Saturday-morning LGBTQIA+ swim squad; asylum seekers finding refuge in a Western Sydney pool; a cancer survivor at Bondi Icebergs.

Whether splashing, paddling, floating or doing serious laps, I muse on race, identity, mental health, nudity, literature, cinema, real estate, ancestors, climate change, sexuality, class, urban design, spirituality, mortality and family.

Intensely personal stories also surface. I write of my two grandfathers – one working class and one patrician – who never met each other but whose fates were both entwined with the harbour, one of them drowning in its waters. I recall my boyhood swimming lessons and reflect on the reckless coastal rites of passage of Sydney teenagers. I describe the respite that swimming in rock pools gave to my mother while she suffered from dementia, rejoice at a barefoot beach wedding, and commemorate a friend whose ashes I scatter in the Pacific.

More than a city guide or a sports book or a collection of meditations and reminiscences, *Swimming Sydney* is a valentine to the beautiful obsession of swimming in the world's most beautiful city. It is a book for everyone who loves swimming, who loves Sydney and who understands that storytelling is the best way to navigate life's emotional currents.

SUMMER

1
RITES OF PASSAGE

SHELLY BEACH, MANLY

My year of swimming Sydney begins on an early-December day. Calendars and media tell me that it's 'summer', but I wonder when summer in Sydney begins and when it ends. After a cool morning, it's become sultry and oppressive. The day's seasonal markers are confusing. Fluffy pale-yellow blossoms of myall wattle hang like Christmas decorations, and the electric-pink flowers of pigface are in full festive bloom. Flathead and coral trout are in the fish shop, and mangoes and berries are on special. Presaging a storm, the sky that started the day as violet has now turned the colour of bruises.

I'm on my way to a wedding in Manly. Two friends have decided to marry on Shelly Beach, and to offer each other their vows with their toes in the sand and the beach as their backdrop.

Arriving half an hour early, I drape my 'wedding clothes' on one of the spare seats that have been set up in the sand at the far right of the beach. Dozens of people, including many international tourists, sunbathe close by or splash at the water's edge. Two young, tanned women – barefoot, but in service black-and-whites – busily set up a drinks table next to the wedding seats, and don't seem at all phased when I ask if they could keep an eye on my clothes and belongings while I jump into the ocean.

The water, made an unusual shade of bottle green by threatening storm clouds, is immediately refreshing, washing away the enervating effects of the day's humidity. I've brought my goggles, so as I swim out towards the coastline's rocks, I'm able to see an amazing abundance of fish darting among the vegetation and between the legs of people treading water. Shelly Beach is part of the Cabbage Tree Bay Aquatic Reserve, which is home to more than 160 species of fish, including protected species such as the weedy or common seadragon, the elegant wrasse and the vulnerable black rock cod. I marvel at how cooling a 15-minute dip can be, and at the utter treat of being able to take an ocean swim half an hour before a wedding. I have a quick shower in the beach's change rooms, get into my glad rags, and ten minutes later begin to chat to other barefoot guests who take their places on the seats in the sand while we wait for the bride and groom.

It is a beautiful, inclusive and moving wedding. For me, the afternoon carries a particular poignancy because I had got to know the bride while we both cared for a mutual friend who was dying of liver cancer. The bride had generously invited me to stand in for our friend who had passed away all too quickly before the wedding.

The wedding begins by acknowledging the traditional owners of Coastal Sydney who, in the words of the couple, have 'loved and wed, in their own way, on the land where we now stand'. The couple thank the original custodians of the land for being such conscientious guardians of this beautiful cove. Near the Fairy Bower car park, 50 metres from where we sit, there is evidence of a large shell midden. Here the Gayemagal people would gather and like us, they would eat and celebrate. And, like me, they would swim.

The relative novelty of a barefoot beach wedding makes

me think that there are few meaningful rituals that are common to Indigenous people and to the colonisers and their descendants. I often wonder why non-Indigenous society has so comprehensively ignored the wisdom that First Nations people have about the area's natural environment, and why we have often failed to integrate any of their practices into our cultural calendars. Non-Indigenous indifference towards Indigenous ways isn't because of any lack of goodwill from First Nations people.

Most Western holidays, such as Easter and Christmas, have their roots in the natural rhythms of the year and have piggybacked on pre-Christian festivals that celebrated things such as a solstice, but none of Australia's festivals seek to connect with Indigenous cultures and the wisdom of the Saltwater Peoples. Why don't Sydneysiders fete the sunny winter days when migrating whales pass by the city's beaches, or acknowledge the time when coastal and riverine flowers first bloom? Why don't we use the Indigenous names for our unique constellations, for more of the fish that swim along our beaches, and for more of the native plants that increasingly resuscitate our thirsty gardens and parks?

As I swim at Shelly Beach and then stand barefoot in the sand at a couple's union, I wonder about how so many of us came to so blatantly ignore or dispel the knowledge that Indigenous Australians have had of Sydney's coastline. I also wonder how we might begin to gain a greater appreciation of the coastal practices and stewardship of Sydney's First Nations peoples. A better sense of seasonal understanding and a truly respectful appreciation of Country could lead us to a deeper understanding of our harbour, our beaches and our waterways. Submerging ourselves in the sea purposefully, mindfully and open-heartedly could build a stronger appreciation of the ocean's recurring gifts and its potential fragility. If we bathe in more ritualised and more contemplative ways, might we begin to approach the kind of spiritual appreciation of the sea that First Nations people have felt so deeply, for so long, in places like Shelly Beach?

Beaches are the places where many rites of passage take place. These rites include losing our virginity, having our first alcoholic drink or taking our first drugs. Yet how often do we go into the water for ceremony, for community, for a sense of greater integration? The coast has been (and always will be) profoundly important to Sydney's First Nations people and to their sense of Country and themselves. Yet for non-Indigenous Australians, the coast's importance largely rests on its recreational value. Perhaps it's time for more of us to immerse and bless our young in its waters, to wed with our ankles in the ocean, and to mourn our dead by the sea.

I feel deeply moved by today's beachside wedding, and I want to know more about the soul, the environment, the history and the stories of Sydney. As I celebrate with the newlyweds and their happy clan, I decide to immerse myself in Sydney's waters and its stories every week for the next year.

2
FRATERNITÉ

CLOVELLY BEACH

Have you ever waited expectantly for a European summer to arrive, only to see June turn to September in an endless string of limp grey days? It's challenging for someone used to the intense blue skies of Australian summers to endure a dud of a northern summer. One of my brothers, Nick, who's spent most of his working life in the Northern Hemisphere, told me how a Parisian summer that never really came left him feeling deeply cheated and oppressed. His lingering sense of summer melancholy was only erased by a late-season getaway to the violet skies and Big Blue of the Greek island of Amorgos. Healed by two weeks of 'hydratherapia', he felt renewed and adequately fortified for another long grey Paris winter.

After 18 years away from Australia, Nick came back to live in Sydney. Shocked by the high cost of housing, appalled by some of the country's mean-spirited politics and feeling a reverse culture shock that can only be understood by those who've lived away for a long time, he cultivated a reacculturation to and growing pleasure in Sydney life by swimming frequently in the ocean. His favourite beach is Clovelly.

Clovelly is particularly popular with Europeans who claim Sydney as home for a month, a year or for decades. With so many beaches to choose from, it's interesting that this one has won their favour. It might be the relative lack of sand, vaguely familiar fishing port topography or serious people-watching possibilities that lure people who are more used to the Mediterranean than the Pacific. It's a strange place: part wharf, part ocean pool, part snorkelling reef, part surf break. I'd not be surprised if a submarine docked at one of its straight-lined perimeters. Its regular squares of concrete slabs were a Depression-era public works project that kept local men in work, and it sometimes puts me in mind of suburban Sydney front gardens in which soil and foliage have been removed and replaced with low-maintenance cement. Viewed from a height on the Bondi to Coogee cliff walk, Clovelly's slabs look like grey fields populated with colourful supine animals.

I'm here today with Nick and, seeing a heaving rainbow of beach towels and bronzed bodies on the patchwork of concrete, we are both reminded of swimming spots in France and Italy and Greece. While there is a small sandy beach at Clovelly's western end, most of the swimmers get wet by jumping off a seawall or descending into the enclosure's usually calm water via ladders. There's no need to make aquatic progress through a barrage of waves. Once wet, people can swim easily here, and for those unnerved by the churning or unpredictable surf of Australia's beaches, this is a big drawcard.

Sixty metres wide and 30 metres long, Clovelly is the largest naturally occurring swimming pool in Sydney. It's ironic that this largest of swimming spaces used to be called 'Little Coogee'. Even on a busy December day, there is room for all to swim, float or snorkel. Sadly, on one such day, a snorkeller who'd had a heart attack and died wasn't noticed as being in distress until his floating body was buffeted up against one of the rocks.

One of the finest things about swimming in Clovelly is its camaraderie. Many swimmers come here to commune with large numbers of fish, and the excitement that this generates is contagious. On several occasions, strangers have waved to me and pointed to something below the water's surface that has delighted them. I've often returned the favour and invited other swimmers into the underwater-loving fraternité. As Nick and I swim a west-to-east length of the long enclosure, we're treated to a submarine parade of life and colour. We swim side by side and as we notice something particularly lovely, we give each other a friendly nudge or poke. Clovelly's generations of blue (and green) gropers are justly famous, as are its populations of wrasse, bream and garfish. All are here in good numbers today, particularly around the rocks at the north-east end of the pool. Clovelly is also home to rock lobsters, abalone, crabs, mussels, oysters and sea urchins. This fish market–worthy haul can't be caught or collected, as the beach is part of the Bronte-Coogee Aquatic Reserve and all its marine life is protected.

After our swim, we lie belly-down on beach towels to chat and dry. Like scores of bodies around us, ours are warmed by the hot concrete from below and by the late-afternoon sunshine from above. In 1902, Clovelly was the first beach in Sydney to legalise mixed swimming in daylight hours. While swimming was tolerated, sunbaking was not. Perhaps to discourage the baring of mixed-gender flesh above the water, change rooms and amenities took a long time to appear. Looking at the g-strings, Speedos and tan lines gracing the beach today, it's hard to believe that such prudish attitudes ever existed.

One of my favourite Australian films is Phillip Noyce's *Newsfront*, and one of my favourite scenes in this nostalgic film has two brothers swimming in Clovelly on a scorching early evening. In nice symmetry with my own brother's experience, one of them leaves Australia to work overseas. The film is more than 45 years old and set 70 years ago, yet the sense of freedom, ease and relief that the two brothers enjoy in the waters of Clovelly is timeless. Perhaps this is what draws me, Nick, and the international fraternity of swimmers and sunbathers to cool off at this strange and beguiling beach.

3
MOONLIGHT

MAHON POOL, MAROUBRA

In the Oscar-winning movie *Moonlight*, the main character – a troubled African American boy – is metaphorically 'baptised' in the sea as he is cradled in the arms of the one adult he trusts. The scene is a moving portrait of waterborne intimacy, and its colours and textures are freighted with emotion. The trusted adult later tells the boy that in the moonlight 'black boys look blue', and for the rest of the movie the colour blue is used to signal the film's emotional turning points.

I think about this scene from *Moonlight* as I take an evening swim at Mahon Pool, a magnificent rock pool north of Maroubra Beach. It's been a horrendously hot day and many people have come to cool down. A large moon is rising over the waves that break beyond the pool. Despite the relatively large crowd, the pool is remarkably quiet. Maybe everyone is too devitalised to talk and can only summon enough energy to surrender to the cooling salt water. Like a community in a Japanese onsen (public bath), the bathers are gently bobbing, stretching and luxuriating, rather than swimming. Many people sit on the rocky rim of the pool, dangling their legs and looking pensively out to the rising moon. It's beautiful to see some young children cradled by adults as they, like the boy in *Moonlight*, float trustingly.

It's not yet fully dark and the lamps illuminating the rock pool turn the sea varying shades of green: depending on where the light hits the water and from which point in the pool I'm in, the water is bottle green, dark jade and grey green. I wonder whether the greens of the sea, like the blues of the movie *Moonlight*, are also emotional triggers. What might people think of as they contemplate this evening's aquatic hues? The moss and weed of coastal pools? The green of vintage beer bottles? The jade stone used for good-luck amulets? The green of a South Sydney Rabbitohs jersey? Childhood memories of overboiled peas?

Cooled and resensitised after a few minutes of floating on my back, I gently breaststroke a few laps of the pool. Negotiating groups and pairs of bathers, I move slowly and am cautious not to break the quiet spell. Underwater, very little life stirs. I've been told that at Mahon Pool octopuses may momentarily peep out from under a rock and then retreat. Octopuses are social and sentient and have the relative intelligence of dolphins or elephants, so I feel great respect for these creatures and am eager not to disturb them.

Like many of Sydney's ocean pools, Mahon Pool was built as a Depression-era employment relief program. Cut out of the rock cliffs at the base of Jack Vanny Reserve, the pool feels more organic and less formally constructed than the rectangular ocean pools further north along the coast. The irregularity of the rocks adds to the evening's sense of gentle embrace and creates a natural gathering point, almost like an amphitheatre from which to view the pool and the ocean beyond. The pool fell into disrepair in the 1980s but, thanks to the persistence of locals, it was renovated and retains its simple rock-shelf enclosures. Twenty-odd wooden posts, each barely a metre high, give a suggestion of a barrier on the pool's perimeter. Linked with steel chains, they remind me of a group of people holding hands and seem a fitting tribute to the locals' love of the pool and their collaborative efforts towards its restoration.

A couple are picnicking on one of the rocks and they gently nuzzle as the last light fades. Eating prawns and sipping wine, they speak softly and quietly giggle as if on a first date. Two cormorants are perched on one of the lampposts, perhaps also expecting a supper of seafood. Effervescent puffs of cooling spray fizz as the waves wash over the barnacled rocks and roll into the pool's eastern side As the night gets darker, the waves announce themselves more by smell, agitation and sound than by colour or shape. They smell like freshly shucked oysters, their ripple is cooling, and they sound like distant thunder. A few hundred metres south of the pool, human voices can just be perceived on Maroubra Beach, but tonight the building sounds of waves refreshing Mahon Pool will erase the murmurs of faraway conversations.

The dozen or so swimmers who remain in the pool have become silhouettes. We no longer display distinguishing features. With our slick heads above the water and bodies below its gently stirring surface, we could all be the same age, the same colour, the same gender, the same size. A sense of awe sits within the pool, and like pilgrims who hush their conversation when entering a dark cathedral, we're honouring something magnificent.

4
'MAY YOU BE WELL…'
MACMASTERS BEACH

I've spent a few Christmases with my brother Mike and his family at MacMasters Beach, and these stays are always a template for a relaxed Christmas by the beach and a full expression of wellbeing. In between feasting on barbecued snapper and prawns and pudding, we laugh and talk and read and doze, and swim in the surf and rock pool. The cicadas hum, the bellbirds tinkle, my niece and nephew play on their guitars and keyboard. After games of Scrabble and walks with Ralph, the resident mutt, members of the family take turns trying on a giant Santa head that looks like something from a European carnival parade.

My family, like many, are at their very best in the days immediately after Christmas. Once the stresses, expectations and preparations of Christmas Day have passed, we give ourselves permission to turn off, relax, reflect, smile and be just that little bit more tender and open-hearted. Unlike most other countries in the world, much of Australia has complete licence to shut down for the final week of the year. It's midsummer and, fed with optimal sunshine, our brains are serotonin-saturated and our loins are stirring. One of three Virgos in my immediate family, I am likely also one of Sydney's many Boxing Day conceptions. Being by the beach at this time of year amplifies the sense of collective exhalation that much of the country experiences. On this afternoon at

MacMasters, I momentarily question if everyone on the beach has been anaesthetised as each single body on its sands is prone and unmoving.

One of the things that makes MacMasters Beach special is that it is bordered by the magnificent Bouddi National Park. Its bushland is like an Australian Arcadia, and it has always reminded me of the dreamlike forest in Sydney Long's Art Nouveau painting *Pan*. Bouddi's delicate angophoras have a magic to them. They arch and twist and dance in the headland's breeze and then cascade down to the surf and rock pool of MacMasters. Bouddi's national park listing was largely due to the efforts of Marie Byles. In the 1930s, she campaigned determinedly with a small group of fellow bushwalkers to ensure the area was saved from development.

Twenty years ago, while riding a bicycle with a friend through the French Concession of Shanghai, I was told the story of Marie Byles. My friend's father had worked with her; she was New South Wales' first female solicitor as well as a mountaineer, adventurer, writer, ascetic and social visionary. Byles, a true bohemian, and a half-century ahead of her time, was also a Buddhist. She periodically meditated in a cave in the Blue Mountains, subscribed to the values of non-violence, and named her Sydney bush retreat Ahimsa – the practice of doing no harm. Byles' life intrigued me and, in researching her Buddhist beliefs, I came upon this mantra: 'May you be well, may you be happy, may you be free from suffering.'

Being mindful involves giving one's attention fully to only one thing. Breath management is a crucial part of this, and the controlled exhalation of one's breath not only stills the mind but also induces a sense of relaxation and a profound state of wellbeing. This Christmas time at MacMasters, I have tried to be more mindful. Allowing myself to register sensations in my body and be more aware of my breath, I feel less distracted and more deeply focused on the beach's beautiful details. During an early-morning swim in its rock pool, I notice little seaweeds underwater that cling to the pool's walls like baby staghorn ferns. The sound of the surf seems louder, the wetness of the sand underfoot seems cooler, the tempo of conversations seems slower. When a local curmudgeon looks at four other swimmers in the rock pool and mutters 'Jeez, it's become Pitt Street!', I laugh rather than take offence and, imagining that I'm part of a pod, enjoy the feeling of the other swimmers' bodies gliding by on either side of me.

On the beach in the days after Christmas, I notice that we all seem to exhale, and I think we become more mindful. We sleep well, we smile, we forgive. We accept past sadness and integrate it into the greater fabric of our lives. We love better, we giggle and we are playful. Our wellbeing is fed by a kindness and gentleness that emanates from this collective exhalation. We are well. We are happy. We are freer from suffering.

5
ANCESTORS

NIELSEN PARK AND
PARSLEY BAY RESERVE,
VAUCLUSE

The Germans, who are at their core a people of the woods, have a word that strongly signifies one's sense of identity and belonging. This word – *Heimat* – doesn't really find an adequate translation into English. It is usually translated as 'home' or 'homeland' but it means much more than this. It connotes strong emotions, sensations and experiences as much as geography. When a German talks about *Heimat*, she or he is also likely referencing an ancestral connection and a collective memory of domestic and regional detail. It's too broad a statement to say that Sydney is my *Heimat*, but I like to think that its salt waters, moving tidally and changing incrementally like history, is where my sense of *Heimat* is most deeply felt.

Other than a brief house-minding stint in Coogee and time with my partner in the Northern Beaches, I have never lived by the coast or in a harbourside suburb. My many Sydney addresses have been in the inner city, south-west, inner west and south, so a salty dip has always been preceded by a (sometimes lengthy) bus, train or car ride. Yet when I am far away and I summon a memory of this city from my inner landscape, my default has me looking across blue water. It is the mental image of the sea that immediately comes to me, rather than terrace houses, native front gardens, Art Deco shopfronts, red-brick flats, BYO restaurants, double-decker trains, multicultural food shops, roads heavy with traffic, cafes that close too early, jasmine tumbling over rear-lane fences, and telegraph poles threaded with garlands of powerlines. All these other images have confronted me many more times, and they are likely much more emblematic of lives lived in Sydney. Yet my 'Sydney' is the sea.

Unlike many suburb-partisan friends, I don't feel at all tribal about where my actual home is. As I look for clues as to why I feel that the city's defining contours of water are my *Heimat*, I'm drawn to Kenneth Slessor's 1939 poem 'Five Bells':

> Where have you gone? The tide is over you,
> The turn of midnight water's over you,
> As Time is over you, and mystery,
> And memory, the flood that does not flow.
> You have no suburb, like those easier dead
> In private berths of dissolution laid –
> The tide goes over, the waves ride over you
> And let their shadows down like shining hair,
> But they are Water; and the sea-pinks bend
> Like lilies in your teeth, but they are Weed;
> And you are only part of an Idea.

The poem is an elegy to an artist who on his way to a party fell overboard from a ferry and disappeared into the depths of the harbour. Lingering forever beneath the water's surface, the drowned artist *becomes* the harbour. The poem was inspiration for one of John Olsen's most celebrated paintings.

Also titled *Five Bells*, it hangs in the Art Gallery of New South Wales. Olsen says that the poem, and his own emotional and physical involvement with the harbour, moved him to try to paint the harbour as 'a movement, a sea suck', and as if he was 'part of the sea'. He wanted to say, 'I am in the sea-harbour, and the sea-harbour is in me.'

Like the elegised character in 'Five Bells', my paternal grandfather fell from a harbour ferry one dark evening and drowned. He died shortly before my father was born and he had lived not far from Nielsen Park in Vaucluse. His experience of Sydney was much more directly lived on and near the water than mine. He swam at Nielsen Park, loved sailing and often took ferries.

My grandfather bequeathed his love of the harbour to his only daughter, Heather, who was 17 years older than my father and, in every sense, a Good-time Girl. Known to us all as 'Cookie', she spoke with a voice made husky from mid-afternoon gins and chain-smoked Ardath cigarettes. She had a volatile nature and an outrageous sense of humour and was married three times. She loved the war years and the American sailors that they brought to Sydney on leave. Spruce and polite Midwestern servicemen carried her handbag, took her dancing, and gave her black-market silk stockings and cigarettes. One of these men got engaged to her before disappearing in the Pacific when his warship was torpedoed. Cookie loved to talk of her adolescent days and nights at Nielsen Park and remained a strong swimmer into middle age. She said the greatest pleasure in life was to lay on its beach under moonlight, slightly drunk, with waves rolling gently over her body.

At about the time that Cookie was lolling at the water's edge, my father was born, and the wonderful 1930s Dressing

Pavilion at Nielsen Park was constructed. A few years ago, I had been touched by a deep and unexpected nostalgia as I entered the Pavilion, ten years almost to the day since my father had died. Open to the elements and referencing Spanish Revival architecture, its change rooms are from an altogether different era and have firmly resisted Sydney's insistence on perpetual renovation. Rows of functional porcelain washbasins and a simple wood-framed mirror speak of cleanliness and dapperness, two virtues my father championed. Dad had grown up in a 1920s block of flats in Bondi and loved the glamour and sophistication of mid-century America. A casting agent, producer and theatrical promoter, he brought Ginger Rogers on tour to Australia and championed the resurrection of King Cross's magnificent Minerva Theatre. The Pavilion strongly spoke to me of the Art Deco idiom, of my father's connections to it, and of a time when Fred Astaire sang to Ginger Rogers of 'moonlight and music, and love and romance'.

Outside the Pavilion stands one of Sydney's most glorious Moreton Bay fig trees. Commanding centrestage in a garden that has a riotous fecundity peculiar to Sydney's eastern suburbs, the fig tree also made me think of my father. Dad was a devout Catholic, but perhaps because he'd lived in Asia as a young man, he also believed that spirits lived in trees. The romantic spirits of Deco-loving Sydney could not find a better home than the Moreton Bay fig tree in Nielsen Park.

In his marvellous biography of Sydney Harbour, Scott Bevan describes gazing to the city from Nielsen Park as not 'so much a view as a vision'. Although I've never lived anywhere near Nielsen Park, I've adopted it as one of the Sydney places that are truly sacred to me, and each visit there is accompanied by a genuine sense of anticipation and wonder. It's almost unthinkable to let a summer pass without at least one swim here. When I lived overseas, I'd return here for family picnics and reunions with old friends, and I'd bring overseas visitors to Nielsen Park to let Sydney show itself off. I've had Christmases on its beach, and romantic, late-summer evening picnics. One year I joined a group of people to stand ankle-deep in its waters and sing songs about the sea as the first light of a January morning lit the sky.

Perhaps because I knew that my grandfather, aunt and father also loved it, I feel deeply at home whenever I walk through the glorious bushland of Nielsen Park and onto the sands of Shark Beach. Sitting on the cement steps of its seawall and looking out to the littoral amphitheatre formed by South Head, Middle Head and Bradleys Head, I have always felt connected to generations of my family. Swimming here is an act of filial piety.

I felt great delight when my nephew, born and reared in France, picked up the nostalgia torch and told me that his visit to Nielsen Park would stay with him for a very long time. Visiting Sydney for a couple of weeks, he'd been taken to the harbour beach on a bright and warm August day and sensibly resisted another uncle's enticements to plunge into the winter waters. However, as the uncle peeled off his own clothes and scoffed at a shivering swimmer coming out of the water ('probably a wimpy European'), my nephew decided to protect the honour of 'wimpy Europeans' and, with nipples burning from the shock of the cold, gallantly swam a length of the beach.

In 2016, the seawall at Nielsen Park was badly damaged by a storm surge. Some sections were repaired, but it was decided that the barrier had reached the end of its 100-year-old life, and remediation work began to future-proof the beach from rising sea levels. Construction of the new seawall was beset by several problems, its completion has run over schedule, and the beach has been closed for successive summers.

Determined to include Nielsen Park in my swim across Sydney and assuming that some portion of the beach could still be accessed, I walked through the gums and fig trees of Nielsen Park and was appalled to discover that Shark Beach, the heritage kiosk and the beach's entire promenade were enclosed in a 2-metre-high security fence. Earthmovers sat atop giant piles of sand, and trenches and pylons ruptured the beach's surface. My harbourside repository of familial memories had been declared a dangerous construction site, and the fence and security cameras ensured that public entrance to the sea was impossible.

Seeing the beach empty of swimmers and imprisoned by a brutal fence, I felt forlorn. It was as if I'd returned to a home that I'd lived in as a child and found it derelict and vandalised, a shell of its former glory. I was relieved that the majestic fig tree was unmolested, and the Dressing Pavilion was essentially unaltered. Most of the Pavilion was locked up but I snuck a quick peep at the men's changing rooms. Except for a carpet of fig leaves, it remained as I had remembered it, and stood dignified among the din and dirt of the construction.

Sitting under the shade of the fig tree, I pondered my choices. I'd wanted to make an aquatic act of filial commemoration here, but the infinitely more pressing needs of the remediation construction work had made that act impossible. It occurred to me that the efforts to mitigate rising sea levels induced by climate change were also, in a way, an act of intergenerational responsibility and respect, ensuring that the children and grandchildren of the people who love this beach passionately can also swim here safely.

Heartened by this realisation, I headed east to nearby Parsley Bay, another heritage swim spot favoured by my grandfather, aunt and father.

Set within a forest of tree ferns, casuarinas, bangalow palms and Port Jackson figs, Parsley Bay Reserve is a glorious and relatively undervisited Sydney jewel. The swimming area is a long, shallow bay and sand flat, flanked by two sandstone headlands that are coated in oyster shells. A striking white suspension bridge runs across the bay. The bridge and the Art Deco kiosk were built in 1929, stylistic companions to the Nielsen Park Dressing Pavilion. Under the water live eleven-armed sea stars, sea lettuce, paddle weed, mud crabs and cockles. A shark net offers safe harbour swimming and seahorses cling to its fibres.

The water is cooling and delicious, washing away my disappointment at discovering that Nielsen Park was an inaccessible mess. I'd thought about my swim at Nielsen Park as a sort of homecoming, but no one was home. Parsley Bay didn't offer the palpable nostalgia I'd sought today, but its harbour waters were essentially the same as those that had caressed my aunt at Nielsen Park and into which my grandfather sank and never resurfaced.

Not long ago I saw a remarkable photograph by Maggie Steber, an American documentary photographer. The photo was titled *Sea of Memories* and it depicted Cuban-born Elly Chovel. Unable to return to Cuba, Chovel purposefully swims in the Caribbean waters that connect the shores of her birthplace with those of her adopted home of Miami. The image of her daily immersion in 'a sea of memories' evokes a sense of profound longing as she reaches in two directions for a *Heimat*. If she cannot ever be fully 'home', she can at least be consoled by the waters that link her past and present.

As I swim at Parsley Bay, I feel like I am also in a sea of memories. I feel I am *of* the water, rather than just in it. The blue-green water is perfectly clear and a school of bream swim underneath me as I do my laps. Like the artist in Slessor's 'Five Bells', I feel time, memories and the 'turn' of the water washing over me. Indifferent to calendar years and linking generations, the waters of the harbour soothe and carry me, and, unexpectedly, make me feel completely at Home.

6

MIRACLES AND GHOSTS

GILES BATHS, COOGEE

The days just after New Year can be a transformative time of the year in Sydney. Having weathered the expectations, emotions and social labour of the festive season, many of us retreat into a lazier space to eat leftovers, rest, laugh and exhale. Early January conversations have a slower tempo, and socialising is less structured. People visibly relax. Giving ourselves permission to simply 'be' can feel miraculous.

For some of us, a ghost might also lurk in the shadows of the first days of the new year. Bereavement or loneliness may be more acute. If someone is absent, their lost companionship can be haunting. Like the dark and empty days that follow the strongly communal rituals of a funeral, the quiet days after the festivities of Christmas and New Year can make us feel numb and bereft. On this afternoon at Giles Baths in early January, I feel a touch of both the miraculous and the ghostly.

Giles is a magical place. Its northern end is enclosed by Coogee's headland and a rock shelf that's the colour of ox blood; its eastern and southern 'walls' are brown-grey sandstone boulders and rocks. Not much separates the swimmer from the open ocean that spills and froths over the eastern breakwater, dramatically rinsing the pool clean and carrying toadfish, garfish, ludericks and crabs into its waters. It is the largest of only three ocean pools in the Sydney region that are made mainly of natural rock. At low tide, it's an aquatic paradise of gently swaying weed, small fluorescent fish and turquoise water. When the tide is high, only the strongest swimmer can lap back through gurgling foam to the east as persistent currents send most of us hurtling towards the shoreline of Coogee Beach.

Bathing for non-Indigenous people began here in what was then called the 'Bogey Hole' in the late 19th century. The baths then became Lloyd's Baths, and while dogs and swearing were forbidden, the men-only baths were advertised as one of the few places 'where the healthful past time of sun baking may be indulged in'. Later, a wooden shack was erected as dressing rooms on the headland above. In 1929, a grander, arched Art Deco building was opened on the headland by Mr OE Giles, offering a swimming pool fed by salt water, and massage, electricity treatments, hydrotherapy and hot sea baths. The sophisticated services in the headland pool drew men from all walks of life, leaving what was to become today's pool to the fish and crabs. Giles' history as a male-only swimming venue, and its clothing-optional sunbaking courtyard, also made it a 'genteel beat' for gay men in the 1930s, 1940s and 1950s.

Giles Baths remained a male-only venue until the 1970s, when violent storms significantly damaged the headland venue and forced its closure. A lone Art Deco archway was all that remained, and it now stands as a memorial to 20 local residents who were killed in the 2002 Bali bombings. Giles' headland, now renamed Dolphins Point, also formally commemorates six members of the Coogee Dolphins, an A-grade amateur rugby league team, who were killed in the bombings.

Wandering around Dolphins Point, it's hard not to feel a sense of sadness and melancholy. Of the 20 people listed on the Bali memorial, none were older than 47 when they died, and the youngest victim was only 14. Some of the victims share the same family names, amplifying the pain and sense of loss that local families must have suffered.

Steps now lead from Dolphins Point down to the rock pool. At high tide this is the only way the baths can be accessed. Today a particular eeriness hangs over the baths as people descend from the headland. Water temperatures have dropped overnight, a result of the 'Ekman transport' effect. Named after the Swedish oceanographer Vagn Walfrid Ekman, the effect refers to a process in which wind moves the top layer of the water and brings significantly colder water from the depths of the ocean up to the surface at the coastline. With the cooler waters also comes a preternatural mist that has spectrally rolled onto the beach like a fog presaging shipwrecks.

Sally, my dear friend and companion today, and I are undeterred by today's fog and see it as an invitation to explore the mysterious. Bravely diving from the rock platform into the clear water without a moment's hesitation, Sally surfaces sleek and smiling and gasps the words, 'That's *fresh!*' I laugh as I more cautiously immerse myself, dipping a foot in and shivering in anticipation.

After the initial shock of the cold, I relax enough to swim several lengths of the rock pool, delighting in the colour and variety of marine life that the nutrient-rich colder waters have delivered. A teenage girl, donning a mermaid fin, joins us. Her encouraging parents film her on a phone as she flips her mermaid tail, and dives down with the grace of Daryl Hannah in the movie *Splash*.

We feel more than invigorated by the swim. The cold Ekman-affected waters have renewed us in a way that feels miraculous. As we climb out of the pool, the January sun begins to burn away the mists and warm our wet skin. With the drops of cold sea evaporating, elation rushes across our bodies and we feel newly alive. Cold water triggers an endorphin that diminishes the body's shock to pain. In her memoir *Turning*, lake swimmer Jessica J Lee talks of opiate users who compare cold water swimming to the effects of heroin. As we laugh with other tingling swimmers and admire the still-submerged mermaid, we feel like we've been given a drug, and its effects are transforming.

The miraculous forces of Giles Baths extend beyond the neurological jolt of a cold swim. For many years, people have claimed that an apparition of the Virgin Mary has appeared on the sea, seen from a cliff-side vantage point just west of Dolphins Point. The spot is easily identified by the rows of flowers, crucifixes, rosary beads and Marian images that have been left by believers near a white fence railing. It makes for an incongruous sight when viewed in front of tanning bathers, the Coogee Bay Hotel and the suburb's blocks of flats. According to information at the shrine, the Virgin first appeared at Coogee on 31 January 2003. Since then, pilgrims dressed in white have come to the shrine once a month carrying a statue of the Virgin. People who claim to have seen her, or had their prayers miraculously answered, have left their petitions and letters of thanks. They come from Vietnam, Lebanon, Nigeria, Iran and Randwick.

Unseasonable mists, Eckman currents, the ghosts of a swim club, a memorial to terror victims. The Virgin watches over all this, and the ebbing tides of Giles Baths keep vigil with her.

7
THE WATER VIEW
GREENWICH BATHS

I begin this chapter with an apology to the long-term patrons of Greenwich Baths, and to the locals who proudly claim it as their neighbourhood pool. I thought I knew coastal Sydney pretty well, but when I stumbled onto these baths, 15 minutes from the city and easily accessed by ferry, train or bus, I was floored. This jewel of a pool is the sort of secret that is jealously guarded by insiders in the know, and who will likely exhale an 'Oh no!' when they see its listing on this book's contents page. I'm sincerely sorry, but your secret is out.

The clichéd phrase 'it's all about the view' is often overused to describe beautiful spots in Sydney, but at Greenwich Baths it *really is* all about the view. A small, netted swimming enclosure, no more than 100 metres long and 50 metres wide, Greenwich Baths has spectacular views south-east across the harbour. Birchgrove and Robinsons Point are in the foreground, with only a yellow-and-green ferry or some moored yachts between them and the swimmers. Beyond Birchgrove, there's Goat Island and the spread of the entire city skyline – Sydney Tower, Barangaroo, the skyscrapers of East Circular Quay. Looking slightly to the right, one can see the cranes and turbine hall of the magnificent UNESCO-listed Cockatoo Island. It's a view that in one glance summarises the history of the inner harbour – pre-invasion headlands of sandstone and eucalypts, stately Victorian homes, industrial maritime dinosaurs, brash 21st-century office towers.

The baths are backed by raked and soft golden sand. There's a stone wall on the left, crusted with sharp oyster shells and topped by gum trees, and a humble wooden-paling fence on the right that separates the baths from multimillion-dollar harbourfront mansions. Apart from a little leaf litter and a stray seagull's feather, the water is clear and fresh. White wooden deckchairs are occupied by novel-reading bathers, and a pile of beach toys is provided free of charge for the littlies. Swish showers, installed in the lower level of a heritage building, provide a civilised post-swim rinse. The upper level of the building houses the very lucky caretaker lessee of the pool, who has the job of opening the baths at dawn and closing them at dusk. Like all good pools, Greenwich Baths has a kiosk that sells hot chips, coffee and icy poles, and plenty of afternoon shade is provided by a leafy north-western garden of fig trees, ferns and pink oleander.

Lolling in the water is as civilised and lovely as lingering on its edges. Four pointed pylons sit in the middle of the enclosure and between them are strung three roped lanes, presumably for swimmers who want to count laps, or for competitions. With so much beauty above and below the water's surface, it seems a shame to be constricted by these lanes and so I opt to breaststroke outside them to make the most of the incredible views. I zigzag backwards and forwards, pointing myself in the direction of anything that catches my eye. Underwater, there's seagrass and more oyster shells and hundreds of tiny fish. I'm delighted by the clarity and the health of the harbour this far away from the Heads. A small tide creates an undulation that encourages my stroke and makes me feel like I'm more a passenger than an active participant in my aquatic motion.

Photographs from the early 20th century show that this area was a makeshift port for local residents' small boats. The colonnade of small upright dinghies that stands sentry at the baths' entrance today maintains some historical continuity. Another charming feature of the pool's entrance is its backyard safety fence that patrons open themselves before paying the small admission fee. Next to the dinghies is *Resignation*, a stone sculpture suggesting a giant chess piece made from sand collected in a plastic bucket. It honours John Spencer Purdy, the Australian chess champion who often swam at the baths.

As I enjoy the water and the setting of Greenwich Baths, I contemplate Sydney's obsession with water views. We'll stand on tippy-toes or lean dangerously out of windows to catch them or claim them as our own; we'll poison trees to improve them; we'll mortgage ourselves to the eyeballs to attain them; and whenever we have them – glimpsed, partial or full – we'll brag insufferably about them. For most of us, they're like the end of the rainbow – we'll never find one because they are now the domain of the historically very lucky or of the stupendously rich. Despite never being able to attain my own water view, I feel grateful to have had such easy and pleasant access to the harbour today. My feeling of gratitude increases as I amble to the Greenwich Point ferry wharf.

Gazing across the breadth of the harbour, I chat to a late-afternoon fisherman whose casting is only minimally interrupted by the arrival of the ferry and a couple of disembarking commuters. I jump on the little boat and, as it meanders across the inner bays of the harbour, I smile at the many mid-week dog walkers, cyclists, beachcombers, picnickers and playing children who use the harbour foreshore as their backyard. They, like me, are enjoying Sydney's many water views.

I notice a JetCat confidently bisecting the western harbour as it cruises towards the Parramatta River. While the views of the Pacific and the harbour are not easily accessed by all Sydneysiders, the city's magnificent rivers – the Cooks, Parramatta, Lane Cove, Nepean, Georges, Hacking, Woronora and Hawkesbury – penetrate and refresh vast areas of greater Sydney. These rivers revitalise suburbia with their wild swimming holes, tidal beaches and calming water views. It occurs to me that even with the city's population growing rapidly, many of us can still enjoy a free water view if we content ourselves with some travelling and with heading back inland to sleep.

8

AT THE MOVIES

MOUNT DRUITT
SWIMMING CENTRE

If there is one thing that I love even more than swimming, it may be going to the movies. I became a cinephile at about the same time that I learned to swim, and both life passions have given me great joy.

I'm not the first person to think that combining water and cinema is a splendid idea. The Flickerfest International Short Film Festival is held annually at Bondi Pavilion. It's the qualifying festival for the Best Short Film and Best Animation categories of the Academy Awards, and an entertaining and intimate evening of beachside cinema. But for sheer fun and exuberance, the best wet movie screenings happen in Sydney's west.

Every January during the school holidays, the Mount Druitt Swimming Centre hosts its family-friendly Saturday night 'Dive-In' movie. For a little more than the regular price of admission to the pool, swimmers get to watch a movie projected next to the main Olympic pool. Mums, dads and kids can relax on lilos, sit poolside and picnic, or splash and play during the boring bits. Past films have appropriately included *Penguins of Madagascar*, *Finding Dory* and *Moana*, but tonight it's *Lightyear*, an origin myth of the Buzz Lightyear character from the *Toy Story* franchise. The film's connection to the water is tenuous, but that really doesn't matter.

Like some of the littlies in the pool, I confess to having flagging attention as the movie screens. Some of this I blame on the predictable plot turns of *Lightyear*, but it's also because I'm more genuinely interested in the cooling ripples of the pool and its audience than the movie.

The swimming centre is a much-loved summer haven for an area of Sydney that can't easily access the coast. Just before its 40th birthday in 2013 it was announced that the pool was not financially viable and would be closed permanently. A new mayor and local activism reversed the decision, and the pool is now thriving, with 30000 visitors swimming here each season. The large grassed areas, landscaping and sun shades temper hot January afternoons, and the swimming pool is a favourite school holiday destination.

Details in the pool's design speak of the area's incredible cultural mix. A striking aquatic-themed mosaic graces the pool's entrance, and its Indigenous motifs announce First Nations claim to the land on which the pool was built and the continued strong Aboriginal presence in Mount Druitt. Within the pool, a series of beautiful social portraits commissioned by the Mount Druitt Ethnic Communities Agency further attest to the cultural diversity and pride of the community. There's a gentle whimsy in the air at Mount Druitt and much credit for this goes to the venue's managers, who creatively use their pool to bring people together in playful and novel ways.

Tonight's 'Dive-In' gets me thinking about the particular pleasures that films featuring swimming, swimmers and the sea offer. Along with Burt Lancaster swimming home in *The Swimmer*, other notable mentions are *Swimming Pool* with Charlotte Rampling, and *A Bigger Splash* with Ralph Fiennes and Tilda Swinton. Pushing human boundaries in the water is a theme that consistently intrigues filmmakers. In *Le Grand Bleu*, competitive free divers risk their lives following the siren call of deep waters, and in *Nyad*, Annette Bening plays Diana Nyad who, at the age of 64 and on her fifth attempt, swims from Cuba to Florida. *Welcome*, the superb and deeply moving story of a Kurdish asylum seeker trying to cross the English Channel to a new life, long stayed in my memory.

Australian cinema is no stranger to the themes of swimming, the beach and water. *Dead Calm* has a yacht-bound Nicole Kidman and Sam Neill fighting for their lives, *Swimming Upstream* has Geoffrey Rush and Judy Davis as the parents of a swimming champion, and *Little Fish* has Cate Blanchett as a lap-swimming ex-addict. Bruce Beresford's *Puberty Blues* has two spirited Cronulla girls rebelling against macho surfie culture, while Simon Baker's *Breath*, an adaptation of Tim Winton's novel, offers a young man's take on surfer bravado and includes some of the best surfing photography to ever grace a feature film.

Mark Twain said that truth is stranger than (cinematic) fiction, and this may be true for what happens to the movie-screening Mount Druitt pool in winter. Incredibly, it is emptied of chlorinated water, refilled with fresh water and 600 live trout from the Snowy River, then turned into a fishing pond for the Family Fish In over the first two weekends in August. For $20, kids (and grown-ups) are given a one-hour spot at one of 50 stations to fish from, and if they're lucky they can take home up to four fresh trout each. Now there's an idea for a Pixar film.

Looking at the kids in Mount Druitt pool whose excitement, like mine, is apportioned between the pool and *Lightyear*, I am touched by their easy interaction and their uncomplicated sense of fun. Perhaps Australia's best movie about swimming remains to be made. Perhaps it involves a group of kids who are full of life and indifferent to difference. Perhaps it is the story of children who share a love of the water, who haven't yet learned to judge or mistrust each other, and who are simply keen to play and splash and laugh.

9

FENG SHUI

GARIE BEACH,
ROYAL NATIONAL PARK

Feng shui literally translates as 'wind water'. If only two words could be used to describe the experience of visiting Garie Beach in the Royal National Park, they should be 'wind' and 'water'. If the wind is still and in harmony with the ocean, the experience of Garie is sublime because its waters are among the clearest and most dazzling in the greater Sydney area. If, however, the winds are stirring, the beach can be challenging. Late summers and early autumns often bring northerly winds, and with them large schools of bluebottles. Unlike metropolitan beaches that are more closely patrolled and signposted, Garie can be wild, and the surprise of a stinger feels scarier without the prospect of immediate first aid. There is very little shelter at Garie, and once the winds whip up flurries of the beach's fine sands, a body basted in sunscreen can quickly become dusted like a freshly crumbed schnitzel. No amount of dousing in the surf can remove this crusting.

In my opinion, Garie is Sydney's most beautiful beach. Long and pristine, it's backed by magnificent moss-green bushland, which is part of the world's second-oldest national park. Cabbage-tree palms and ferns grow heartily, cicadas noisily whir from the twisted red-brown limbs of coastal gums, and at sunset, deer and wallabies may nervously appear at the point where the sand meets the bush. At the northern end of the beach, a craggy crimson headland dramatically breaks away. At the southern end lies a myriad of tidal pools stirring with life and festooned with white and green barnacles.

Garie has frequently cast a healing spell for me. My oldest brother Steve and his family live close by, and the beach has been a major meeting place for us over the years. Prostrated on beach towels or splashing in the surf, we talk and laugh and nurture familial bonds playfully and effortlessly. When I was living in densely urban Hong Kong, I'd often visit Garie on return visits to Sydney during the Lunar New Year holidays. Garie felt like Hong Kong's polar opposite, and the sense of wellbeing generated by its natural beauty and expansiveness was a great way to mark a new year in the Chinese calendar. Chinese feng shui masters believe that the most auspicious places look towards water and are backed by hills. Garie's geography is graced with this favourable combination, and it was greatly anticipated and keenly missed when I was in my small Hong Kong apartment. I once brought a Hong Kong friend to Garie and her immediate reaction was telling: 'What a wonderful place to grow old in!' she exclaimed.

My father had lived in Hong Kong as a young man and always loved returning to its colour, verticality, chaos and energy. He enjoyed the astonishment and envy that older Chinese people expressed when he told them that he had five sons. He also loved the emphasis on rituals that attended family gatherings. He nicknamed me 'Marco Christopher' because of my frequent travelling, and when I was visiting from Hong Kong, he was happy that I made time each summer to ceremonially be with Steve and his family at Garie. Dad loved the filial affection that accompanied our accounts of a day at the beach. Hearing about our swims at Garie was, for him, as good as being there himself, and knowing that two of his sons were enjoying the same day together made it doubly special. Dad worked as a record producer, theatrical agent, concert promoter and filmmaker, but he often boasted with a smile that his 'greatest productions' were his five sons.

Garie was where Steve and I came soon after the death of our father. Likely still in shock and numbed by grief, we found that things didn't need to make sense as we waded into the pale-blue surf and let the Pacific wash away some of our distress and sadness. The wind cooled us, the water cleansed us, and the environment seemed to offer a dignified consolation. After the swim, I felt more at peace with my thoughts, feelings and memories.

Another new year in the Chinese calendar has begun, and Steve and I mark it by making a special effort to get to Garie. A wild storm more than a year ago created a landslip in the Royal National Park and the road to the Garie Beach car park has since been off limits. The only way to the beach is via the strenuous but beautiful Curra Moors track. When we arrive at Garie, we're greeted by fresh winds and sparkling water, hopefully auspicious signs for a year of peace, good health and contentment. As I surrender myself to the breakers, I carry these hopes in my heart. Diving under a wave, I hold my breath and think of all I love.

10

'ALWAYS WAS, ALWAYS WILL BE'
VICTORIA PARK POOL, CAMPERDOWN

One evening during an event at the Sydney Town Hall, a sublime digital artwork depicting Sydney, pre-invasion, was screened as part of the Welcome to Country. The video drew gasps from the audience, and I felt goosebumps as it unfolded. Meticulously crafted by Kooma man Brett Leavy and the team at Virtual Songlines, a digital design company, the video's virtual time machine took us to a Sydney before European contact and asked us to reimagine places that we thought we knew with fresh eyes and an open heart. Bennelong Point, Pitt Street Mall, Farm Cove and George Street were shown as dense bushland, undulating sandstone rock shelves, fresh waterways and land rich in fauna. At the end of the video, my friend Charmaine turned to me and, with tears in her eyes, said, 'I can never see Sydney again in quite the same way.'

I'd had a swim at Victoria Park Pool earlier in the day that I'd seen the video. Wanting to know more about the pool and its unique location between the major city arteries of Parramatta Road and City Road, I'd read about the history of the pool's site and was astonished to discover that Victoria Park was originally Blackwattle Creek, a tidal watercourse that once extended towards Redfern and Waterloo. Following European occupation, the creek's precinct was variously transformed into a waterhole, a farm, a military camp, a horse pond, a dam, a grand approach to a university, a launch pad for hot air balloons and, finally, a park that enclosed Northam Lake and the swimming pool.

In the middle of Northam Lake sits a fountain and a bronze sculpture of the boat *Barrenjoey*, commemorating the gold medal for yachting that was won by Sydney local councillor William Northam and his teammates at the Tokyo Olympics in 1964. 'Barrenjoey' is said to mean 'young kangaroo', and no doubt many of these roamed here before the lands were cleared. There's conjecture that Parramatta Road and King Street in Newtown, which border Victoria Park, were once Indigenous walking tracks. Like many other main streets in Sydney, their contours may have mirrored Indigenous boundaries and thoroughfares, and their 21st-century traffic may be following the pathways of First Nations people. When I spoke to Brett Leavy, he said that these walking tracks and trade routes were 'deliberately and organically constructed to follow the natural landscape and were the transport routes that connected First Nations settlements before European settlement'. Once the colonial boundaries expanded, development of roads and tracks followed the usual grid pattern, mirroring those of planned cities in Europe and America to create a more orderly and efficient urban environment. Yet Sydney's initial layout was shaped by its harbour and hilly terrain, and, according to Leavy, follows 'the ancient routes and songlines established and used by the First Nations people since time immemorial'.

Victoria Park Pool is an island of water in a sea of park. The pool is a relative newcomer to the site. It was built in 1953, one of 25 in-ground public pools that were part of a postwar building frenzy in Sydney. After the war, it became compulsory for all primary school children in New South Wales to learn to swim, and pools like Victoria Park were constructed to task this requirement. The pool had its 15 minutes of fame in 1975 when the band AC/DC played on its roof.

Architecturally, the pool today hasn't changed greatly since the 1950s. Its old-school bones evoke a time when childproof fences and occupational health and safety were mere twinkles in a council member's eye. The small square tiles lining the bottom of the pool are porcelain and shiny, and some are yellowing in places. At the eastern end of the pool, below its eight raised starting blocks, the water suddenly deepens to 3 metres. The pool's perimeter is lined in gravy-brown tiles, and its cemented areas, designated for sunbaking, gave no consideration to sun protection when they were laid out.

Today, thanks to the love and funding of the City of Sydney, the pool is heated during winter, and it boasts elegant sunshades, a friendly gym and retrofitted change rooms. Groups of wetsuited trainees learn scuba diving in the deep end, men in colourful budgie smugglers flirt with each other on the terrace, and international students from the University of Sydney do laps between lectures in the pool's wide lanes. Despite these social changes, the pool's defining feature – a direct connection to the park's palms, fig trees, lawns and birds – is also as it was in the 1950s, and this makes it a special urban oasis.

As I swim in the clear water on this sparkling late January afternoon, I look beyond the contours of the pool to the park that encloses it. I think about all the people who, over the years, have dozed beneath a fig tree, sat on the grass and swatted for an exam, stolen a kiss, yelled at a scavenging ibis or just daydreamed. When researching the park's history, I'm surprised by old black-and-white photos from the early 20th century. They show dense tree cover, trams barrelling down

City Road, and ladies in hats and gloves promenading. In these photos, the neo-Gothic towers of the university, spooky and not fully distinct, are perched on a hill like a Transylvanian castle, and they retain pride of place as I look westwards today.

The park and the pool have been an urban junction for many years, and I believe that an essence of the lives lived in and around the park has somehow been captured and stored by the trees that surround me. My friend Charmaine is a great lover of all things arboreal and someone who, with growing age and wisdom, has developed an intense affinity with trees and plants and flowers. I had a conversation with her one evening about the possibility of us all ending up in the trees where we live. She wondered aloud whether we, as carbon-based life forms – like possums and flying foxes and kookaburras – are released into the atmosphere as carbon when we die and decompose. Trees capture liberated carbon to build and nourish new life, so could it be that developing a stronger affinity with trees is the first hint of the fact that one day we will all, in a sense, become trees?

The trees that I look at from the pool are relatively young. Most were planted a mere hundred years ago, or even more recently. Their arboreal predecessors were the native tamarind, white cherry, lilly pilly, blackwood, rough tree fern and cheese tree. As part of a rainforest that existed here for thousands of years, whose carbon did they capture and protect until they were cleared to make way for the farm, the military camp, the park and the university that the colonisers built?

In the south-east corner of Victoria Park sits a wooden Canadian totem pole. One of only a few in Australia, it is a significant example of Canada's indigenous heritage, and was carved by Hwunumetse', also known as Simon Charlie, from the Cowichan Nation, Coast Salish. It was given to the city of

Sydney in 1964 by the Canadian government on the occasion of National Timber Week. I can't but gasp at the irony of the presence of this indigenous sacred object on the site of a cleared rainforest.

In Victoria Park on 26 January, people come together for the Yabun Festival, Australia's largest one-day celebration of the survival and thriving resilience of Aboriginal and Torres Strait Islander cultures. The festival showcases fantastic music, dance, ideas, leadership and community, and it animates the continuity between traditional and contemporary Indigenous cultures. The pool, free to kids for the day, is a place of great playfulness on the usually hot January day, and it becomes a focal point of the festival. Yet as high-vis-vested council workers clean up after the festival and the regular swimmers take back the pool, any comprehensive and physical remembrance of the ancient relationship of First Nations peoples with the land is put into storage for another year. The land that we know as Victoria Park always was and always will be Aboriginal land, but nothing about the landscaped park, the statue of a boat commemorating an Olympic gold medal, the Canadian totem pole or the well-appointed swimming pool reminds us of this for 364 days of the year.

11

DOG PADDLES AND PLUTO PUPS
LEICHHARDT PARK AQUATIC CENTRE

Today has brought me back to the Leichhardt swimming pool for the first time in more than 50 years. What is now the Leichhardt Park Aquatic Centre was where I learned to swim as a six-year-old.

Because of my father's sometimes peripatetic career in the entertainment industry, we moved around a fair bit when I was a kid. Before we moved into the home that would be the setting for most of my boyhood – a little weatherboard-and-fibro house in Campsie – we lived for a time in a run-down, two-storey mansion in Johnston Street, Annandale. The neo-Gothic house had been bought by my great-grandmother during World War II, and its once-grand living spaces were converted into hastily built, gimcrack flatettes during the 1940s housing shortage. Little about the house had changed by the time we moved in 30 years later. Our mercurial great-aunt, who bore more than a passing resemblance to Miss Havisham, had inherited the house many years previously, and when she wasn't drinking in the ladies' lounge at the nearby Empire Hotel, she was watching a black-and-white television in her 1940s kitchen.

Our family lived in the flat on the top floor of the house. As a six-year-old, I shared a bedroom with my parents while two brothers slept in bunk beds on a landing, and another two shared a double bed at the back of the flat. The kitchen and bathroom still had gas meters, and a hot bath required a 10-cent piece. As well as our great-aunt and her husband, the house accommodated my grandfather, and two lodgers – an alcoholic former merchant sailor who had a liking for Bex powders (and, we suspected, our great-aunt), and a communist retired wharfie.

It's almost a cliché to say that 'life was simpler then', but it was. Although it was the early 1970s, life in our corner of Annandale felt more Ruth Park than Gough Whitlam. We knew neighbours and local business owners by their names, went to the back door of a local lolly factory to beg for free sweets, and fought over whose turn it was to burn the rubbish in the backyard incinerator. I walked myself to and from school, and if we were lucky enough to be given some coins, we bought bags of mixed lollies and potato scallops from the shops on Parramatta Road. In the early evenings, as she prepared dinner for seven people, my mother would often put a green two-dollar note in my hand and send me up to the local pharmacy to buy 'Peter Stuyvesant cigarettes and a packet of Modess'.

On the weekends, my brothers and I stalked what was then a very working-class Annandale in search of adventures. Once we scaled a barbed wire fence to scurry up a ladder and climb to the slate roof of the local Anglican church, admiring the view from the high sandstone turret. Occasionally, we broke into the lolly factory, clambering over palettes of boxed sweets, exploring the factory's industrial mysteries and dipping a finger into vats of toffee mix. In the school holidays, we saw James Bond films (and the occasional rat) at a local cinema, supported the Balmain Tigers (who our grandfather had played with in the 1920s) and swam at Leichhardt pool.

Sometimes my mother would join us at the pool. She'd

prepare a picnic of boiled chicken and salads of iceberg lettuce, tomatoes and canned beetroot – sensibly carried on the bus in old plastic ice cream containers – and we'd eat on the pool's lawns or at its wooden picnic tables. We'd bomb and splash, hop on the hot poolside cement, and beg Mum for a pluto pup (a battered, deep-fried sausage on a stick) from the kiosk. She loved the anarchy of young sons and would laugh and daub our noses with zinc cream.

One summer holiday, I was enrolled in swimming classes at the pool. Wanting to keep up with my older brothers, I'd already taught myself the basics of staying afloat. I'd also vaguely remembered wearing a styrofoam 'Pixie Bubble' flotation device when I was very little, so I felt no anxiety being in the water. Our beginners' swimming class involved doing a safety jump from the deep end (arms held straight out in a T shape, feet together), learning to tread water and then dog-paddling the width of the pool. By the end of the week, I had my water safety certificate, and for much of the rest of that summer I was dog-paddling madly with my brothers.

In between splashing in water that was likely cleansed with industrial-strength chlorine, we sucked on Glugs and Razzes, and on Sunnyboys – pyramid-shaped frozen treats that were luridly coloured and contained absolutely no natural ingredients. They were 5 cents each and wrapped in a foil that disintegrated as the ice treat melted. The foil's lining sometimes contained orange writing on its inside that offered a treat for free. Aspiring confidence tricksters, my brother Mike and I once unsuccessfully tried to use an orange texta to forge the writing and claim a freebie from the swimming pool kiosk.

No one spoke seriously of sun protection in the 1970s, and we were regularly so sunburnt after a day at the pool that we'd blister and, later, shed skin onto our cotton sheets like snakes. Nowadays, knowledge about the sun's potential danger, general pool safety and ideas about lifelong fitness have changed enormously, and these have prompted some of the most striking differences at Leichhardt pool.

In what is now known as the Leichhardt Park Aquatic Centre, a gym has been added, as have sun shelters, a creche and a small indoor pool. However, the pool's 1960 build is still very evident: the main Olympic pool with its border of blue-and-white tessellated tiles, the red-brick changing sheds, and the diving pool with its three aqua-and-pink cement diving platforms are much as I remember them. The tuckshop is in the same place but has been enlarged into a sophisticated cafe serving gluten-free muesli, halloumi rolls, piccolo lattes and booster smoothies – fare entirely foreign to 1970s Sydney. While pluto pups and Sunnyboys are no longer on offer, hot chips, Drumsticks and icy poles can be still bought as after-swim treats. Unchanged too are the lawns and picnic tables where we ate Mum's salads, and the common areas with their yellow and crimson and grey patchwork cement, where we burned our young skin and ran, hot-footed, despite the lifeguards' protests.

The pool reminds me of the 1950s outdoor pools in the inner suburbs of Brisbane. I was delighted to discover these pools when I visited close friends there, and thought that Sydney, ever renovating and redeveloping itself, had few similar aquatic charmers. The impression I have of being in Brisbane is accentuated by today's high humidity, and by the huge fig trees around nearby Leichhardt Oval. Birdlife, including ibises and corellas who feed in nearby Iron Cove, are drawn to the area by its foliage and revitalised mangroves. The birds and grand trees add to the languid sense of nature that very much defines Brisbane, and the avuncular staff further make me feel like I've crossed the Queensland border.

It seems like I'm not the only person who feels enormous nostalgia when I visit this pool. Stephen, a local resident, artist and friendly pool employee tells me that there has been a collective outpouring of sadness in response to the news that the diving tower (now closed) has been diagnosed with concrete cancer and will likely be demolished. Like me, many other local children made their first grand leap into a deep pool from the tower and now, many years later, they see its removal as yet another instance of the erasure of physical space as memory. With the loss of shared public space, collective memories also disappear. Stephen passionately advocates for the protection of recreational public places, musing that as 'we lose places where we can be egalitarian, we also become more fractured as a society'.

This afternoon, various after-school swim groups are in full swing. Some of the children are learning to swim and others, now more than competent, are racing in squads. I look sentimentally at lane 3, where I first did a safety jump and paddled like a retriever. As the kids splash and squeal and glide on either side of me, I slide into lane 3 to swim some laps and enjoy some aquatic nostalgia. As I climb out of the pool, a gaggle of giggling children catch my eye, their hair slick from the water and their faces rosy from activity. They're about the same age I was when I learned to swim all those years ago. Walking to the change rooms, I smile at them, wish them fun, and hope that they can come back here in half a century's time.

12
STORM CLOUDS

COCKATOO ISLAND

The words 'late summer' often conjure up an image of hot and dry times, but Sydney in February can be sweltering and unpredictably sultry. As I wait for a ferry to Cockatoo Island, an electrical storm is brewing. With time to kill, I sit in the park next to the Museum of Contemporary Art and enjoy some of the natural delights that accompany these humid days. Gymea lilies are in bloom, dianella berries have appeared, and Port Jackson fig trees are bearing fruit. Eastern koels, recognisable by their red eyes and their blue-black sheen, are darting among the native trees.

I board a little yellow-and-green ferry with scores of other daytrippers, and for 30 minutes we bounce across a choppy harbour that is turning inky purple from the gathering storm clouds. We arrive on the northern side of Cockatoo Island. Situated geographically and historically in the middle of Sydney Harbour, the harbour's largest island exerts a loud and powerful presence. It is an extraordinary site for musing on the harbour's contested history. It was about this time of year that the colonisers first arrived in Sydney, perhaps on a day very much like today. Australia Day has just passed and as we grapple with reconciliation and how to best celebrate our national identity, it seems fitting to reflect on our harbour's histories on an island that belonged to First Nations peoples before it became a convict prison, an industrial shipyard, and a hub for art and ideas.

Cockatoo Island is a mammoth lump of sandstone and, like potter's clay, it has been shaped and reshaped by Sydney's governing classes. Red gums draped the sandstone outcrop and the cockatoos that lived in them inspired the British to give the island its name. In the 1830s and 1840s, Cockatoo Island was used by the British as a lock-up for reoffending convicts. The prison was a notoriously brutal place, and convicts were forced to manually carve wheat-storing silos out of the island's solid cliff walls, forever disturbing its natural balance. Like on Alcatraz, that other famous prison in the middle of a beautiful harbour, escape stories were legendary and the only prisoner to successfully escape was a 'gentleman bushranger' who later went by the name of Captain Thunderbolt. His infamy, and the ghostly presence of tortured and abused convicts, hang heavily over the island's forlorn sandstone barracks.

Colonial Sydney had a knack for using convict labour to serve commercial interests and Cockatoo Island was no exception. It housed a black-market cabbage farm and later became the colony's shipbuilding centre. Convict gangs hacked away rock to make way for docks and slipways, and when the Sutherland Dock was built on the south-western side of the island in 1890, it was the biggest dry dock in the world. The island's population was overwhelmingly masculine, with one exception. As well as being a gaol and shipyard, Cockatoo Island housed a girls' reformatory. Girls under 16 who had committed a crime, engaged in 'at-risk' behaviour such as begging or vagrancy, or were found in the company of prostitutes or thieves were detained here. They became de facto slaves and there was evidence that some girls had their heads shaved, were confined to unlit rooms and were physically maltreated.

The island's bifurcated history of penal brutality and maritime industry is physically evident in the UNESCO World Heritage–listed built structures. Rusting cranes and a giant turbine hall take my breath away as I walk around them. They stand like obelisks and abandoned cathedrals, consecrated to the patron saints of industry. For most of the year they are bereft and cavernous, their darkness and silence broken only by the fluttering of a seagull or the footsteps of a tourist. After being decommissioned as a shipbuilding site at the end of the last millennium, the island became a venue for the Biennale, Sydney's pre-eminent international contemporary art event. I think of the chilling context that the soaring, derelict turbine hall gave to a monumental work by Chinese artist Ai Weiwei at a previous Biennale. Ai's work was an enormous rubber sculpture representing refugees hanging precariously onto a dinghy in stormy weather. Set in a ghostly space on an island known for prison savagery, immigrant labour and maritime activity, the work exuded a majestic irony and a lingering sense of tragedy.

In 2000, an Aboriginal rights group, led by Wiradjuri woman Isabel Coe, set up a Tent Embassy on Cockatoo Island and filed a native title claim, contesting British sovereignty over the island that was called Wareamah by its original owners. Indigenous activists claimed that 'there is an Aboriginal title to the land which pre-dates the title of the Commonwealth of Australia and which has not been extinguished' and that the island was 'the joint property of all aboriginal people, not the property of any individual clan or family now extinct'. Their claim ultimately was unsuccessful, but discussions of sovereignty continue.

On the west-facing side of the island, there is a swimming enclosure of sorts. It's not an official enclosure like Marrinawi Cove in Barangaroo, but its immediate access to the harbour is similar – and compelling. The enclosure is accessed by a derelict concrete slipway, made precarious by years of seagull guano. I question the wisdom of this swim. For many years, industrial waste flowed from the shipyards and, looking up to an abandoned steam-powered crane and a towering brick chimney, I feel like I'm submerging myself in a factory's cooling system rather than the harbour. The guerrilla swim is brief and furtive, but unlike any other I've done. There's a ghostliness to this human-built space, and the relics of prisons and commerce are at odds with the magnificent natural setting. I try to acknowledge the full power of the island's history: the displacement of First Nations people and the remnants of the Tent Embassy; sandstone convict barracks; and towering industrial dinosaurs from a long-gone maritime age. My head and heart are overwhelmed by the history of this place, and I am fatigued by its harsh stories.

The slipway suddenly drops off and I'm chest-deep in salty water. Though the harbour here is scuzzy, I find it soothing as its ebb and flow commands my attention. As I stretch out and swim towards the enclosure's netting, I feel like I am letting go of the island's dark history and focusing instead on the water rippling around me. With my back to the buildings, my attention turns more fully to the squawk of seagulls, the battleship greys of storm clouds above, and the smell of frangipani flowers that grow on the island's huge and venerable trees. Weather and nature holds sway over me and I surrender to their thrall.

13
THE SWIMMING POOL LIBRARY

ANDREW 'BOY' CHARLTON POOL, SYDNEY

There is no more seductive urban public swimming pool in Sydney than 'the Boy'. In fact, the Andrew 'Boy' Charlton Pool is quite possibly the world's most glamorous public swimming pool.

Barcelona's Piscina Municipal de Montjuïc, made famous by Kylie Minogue and dozens of impossibly beautiful writhing bodies in the 'Slow' video, certainly deserves a notable mention. As does Badeschiff Berlin, a shipping-container-turned-infinity pool that floats in the river Spree in east Berlin. Populated by urbanites sipping Aperol spritzes, lolling in deckchairs or moving to the tunes of the pool's resident DJs, Badeschiff is most definitely uber-cool. But to my mind, neither of these give 'the Boy' a true run for its money for gob-smacking public-pool beauty and sexiness. Singer-songwriter Loudon Wainwright III agrees with me; in a *New York Times* article, he named the pool as one of the ten best places on the planet to swim. French-American Olympic swimmer Casey Legler, burnt out and not having swum for 20 years, was lured back to the water after laying eyes on this gorgeous pool.

Bordered on three sides by Sydney Harbour, and the Botanic Gardens on its fourth, The Boy's greatest asset is its communion with Mother Nature in Woolloomooloo Bay. Like the swimmers in its lanes, the pool itself is lodged in the water, sitting on pylons above the lapping blue-greys of the harbour. Entering the pool feels like boarding a ship: one literally crosses a gangplank to pay admission and then descends a flight of maritime metal stairs to the terraced pool area. A pontoon below the main pool groans as it bobs up and down with the tides, and this makes me further feel that I'm on the water as well as in it. It's an astonishing pool to swim in, and, doing breaststroke to maximise the incredible views from the most easterly lanes, it feels as much like sightseeing as swimming. Between breaths as I swim north, I can see the harbour, Garden Island, Manly ferries, and the Moreton Bay figs and sandstone of Mrs Macquaries Point. Doubling back and heading south, I see Woolloomooloo's heritage-listed Finger Wharf, the yachts of the rich and famous, and the navy ships and Art Deco apartments that call Potts Point home.

On a dazzling late-February morning that also happens to be Mardi Gras Saturday, the Boy feels more resort or clubhouse than municipal pool. Bronzed bodies recline on the pool's many sunbeds or sip cool drinks among the potted east-west palms of the pool's cafe. Sensuality floats over the pool's eight lanes, and competing with the sounds of muscled limbs splashing are the raucous squawks of cockatoos. Lane markers are blue and white, like the stripes of a matelot's shirt. They echo the nautical mood created by the many battleships moored in the bay, adding to the *Querelle of Brest* homoeroticism that is often evident at this port city pool. The only slug in this salad of sensual delights is the extreme saltiness of The Boy's water. Every time I dive into it, I am surprised by how salty the pristine pool is, and I feel like I'm licking the foil wrapper from a packet of Smith's crisps.

I recall Booker Prize–winner Alan Hollinghurst's first novel, *The Swimming Pool Library*, whenever I go to the Boy. Its title and primary metaphor evoke men swimming together, in what *New York Times* reviewer Catherine Stimpson described as 'an eroticized, romanticized male community that myth and history, art and nature can cherish'. On most days, 80 per cent of the swimmers at the pool are men, so the Boy is about cruising as well as swimming. One day after a swim, I noticed a naked man with an impish grin and an erection circulating in the pool's stylish subterranean change rooms. Unconcerned or smiling amusedly, the other guys got on with the business of changing and showering, or teasingly lingered.

Today the glamour index at the Boy hovers between high and extreme. A cluster of buff men with topknots, oiled six packs, trimmed beards and tattoos fraternise and strut. Wearing aussieBum swim briefs, men in smaller groups recline on Missoni beach towels and check their phones with insouciance. The whites of AirPods and the dark frames of Ray-Ban aviator glasses accentuate the gold of their handsome tanned faces. In my sensible grey rashie, Cancer Council sunnies and Akubra, I feel, by contrast, more queer fish than Queer. It seems that no one is in a hurry, an anomaly in this often time-poor city.

Andrew Charlton is the perfect namesake for this venue. Athletic and handsome, he was one of Australia's first golden boys of swimming. At age 16, he thrillingly defeated the world's best swimmer, Swede Arne Borg, in this pool, and then beat him again at the 1924 Paris Olympics, winning the gold medal in the 1500 metres freestyle. In Paris, Charlton also competed against American hunk Johnny Weissmuller, who would later become Hollywood's first Tarzan and who would not look at all out of place at the Boy today.

The Boy has a venerable history. The sheltered bay in which it is located was used as a bathing place for millennia by the Gadigal people, and after the colonisation of the area, convicts, military personnel and civilians bathed in the area, which was called the Fig Tree. The city's first free public baths were built here in 1858. At the beginning of the 20th century, the baths were enlarged, embellished with Edwardian turrets and latticework, and named the Domain Baths or 'the Dom'. In 1968, when the Dom was demolished and rebuilt as an Olympic-sized pool, the new pool took the moniker of the Olympic champion who had swum there. The first Mardi Gras gay and lesbian swimming carnival was hosted here in 1985, and the February night-time event continued for 16 years.

As Sydney pulses with pre–Mardi Gras fever this year, the Boy also heats up. Abs are chiselled, tan lines are darker, and swimmers flirt with a sweet breeziness. But Mardi Gras is also about community, and this is consistently expressed by the LGBTQIA+ swimming club, Wett Ones, who meet here on Saturdays at 9.30 am to train, support each other and socialise.

The 'Wetties' who are swimming today greet me with smiles, handshakes, and an easy and genuine inclusion. Some of the swimmers have been with the group for 20 years; others are relatively new recruits. They range in age, body shape, ethnicity and swimming ability, but all share a love of the water. Wett Ones currently has about 180 active members and is not only the largest LGBTQIA+ swim club in Australia, but also the largest masters swimming club in New South Wales. They race in competitions through Masters Swimming Australia, and their swimmers consistently sit at the top of the rankings. Many of the swimmers have successfully competed in the Gay Games, but while competition is very much supported and nurtured, swimmers who want to exercise or improve their stroke are also catered to. Coaches tailor swim routines for swimmers of different levels, and the lane I've joined today soon has me doing freestyle, backstroke, rolls, and free form (any stroke other than freestyle). I'm gently pushed a little harder than I might otherwise swim but there's no sense of coercion or pressure. At the end of each set there's a brief chat, more smiles and lots of encouragement. I'm told that other swim meets happen throughout the week at the Sydney Uni Sports & Aquatic Centre pool, Prince Alfred Park Pool, the Ian Thorpe Aquatic Centre and Victoria Park Pool.

By the time I've left the pool, showered and am sipping a coffee with other swimmers at the glorious poolside cafe, I feel like a million dollars. Talk is turning to tonight's Mardi Gras parade and some group veterans recount previous Wett Ones Mardi Gras floats. It seems that most years a squadron of Speedo-ed, body-painted Wetties do an elaborate piece of shimmy-and-stroke choreography, providing a huge sugar hit of eye candy.

As the Wetties head home to rest before the evening's fun and celebrations, each one invites me to join them for more swimming. I'm touched by their friendliness and inclusion. Socially immersed in this most likeable aquatic group for a morning, I also feel like I've become a member of something wonderful: something akin to a swimming pool library.

AUTUMN

14
GRANDFATHERS

WATSONS BAY

Both my grandfathers' lives were largely defined by Sydney Harbour.

My mother's father, known to everyone, including his grandchildren, as Harry, was a working-class man from the shipyard foreshores of Balmain. Harry left school at 13, fathered a child as a teenager, and then went to the Western Front as an underage soldier. He worked for many years as a boilermaker at the Garden Island naval dockyard. Though he worked hard and never amassed any savings, he lived a long and mostly happy life.

During World War II, Harry was involved in Australia's greatest shipbuilding and repair program, in which three crews of workers laboured for 24 hours a day to build, refit and repair navy vessels. The program took on enormous urgency after Japanese midget submarines entered Sydney Harbour in 1942 and fired torpedoes into Garden Island. One unexploded torpedo landed not too far from where Harry worked. A week later, more midget submarines fired airborne shells into the eastern suburbs and, again, an unexploded torpedo landed close to where Harry and his family rented their modest semidetached house.

Despite his difficult early life and his scrapes with wartime drama, Harry remained a gregarious man with a legion of friends across Sydney. He moonlighted as an SP bookie, and on race days when his earnings were especially good, he'd celebrate by buying a box of fresh fruit for his wife and second daughter, before taking the family to 'The Pictures'. When he had the time, Harry relaxed by fishing at Watsons Bay.

In her novel *Seven Poor Men of Sydney*, Christina Stead (a long-time resident of Watsons Bay) captures the village atmosphere and social spectrum of the area in the 1920s. A passage from the book that has long stayed with me is a description of snotty-nosed waifs wading into the harbour with hessian bags to collect stray pumpkins and pieces of coal that had fallen off overloaded transport barges.

Symbolic of the mixing of social classes that occurred in Watsons Bay for much of the 20th century, Harry the boilermaker often went out fishing with his mate Mick Doyle, a family member of the Doyles fish and restaurant empire. Like the small weatherboard fishermen's cottages of Watsons Bay that still sit next to the modern houses of social grandees, Harry and Mick sat together in a dinghy, swapping stories as they fished, and continued the banter over beers in the Watsons Bay Hotel. One of the great treats that my brothers and I enjoyed during our boyhoods was being taken to this Art Deco pub by Harry. Proudly introduced to Mick and Harry's other friends ('This little fella is number five!'), I'd sit on the front pub's step or on Harry's lap, greedily slurping a lemon squash through a paper straw as the men swapped stories and laughed.

On hot summer days in the early 1970s, my lemon squash would be preceded by a swim in the Watsons Bay Baths. These boyhood dips involved paddling out towards the greater harbour and thinking about its potential dangers as I looked to the boats, incoming ferries and the Harbour Bridge. While the wooden diving tower and mesh shark nets of the enclosure gave some sense of comfort and safety, swimming in the sometimes murky, often busy working waterways of the harbour felt more reckless and fraught than a swim in the open surf. In his wonderful history of Sydney Harbour, journalist Scott Bevan gives some credibility to my shark fears by noting that as a boy, the writer Robert Drewe also swam within the shark enclosures of the bay and discovered that they were full of large holes.

Despite welcome 21st-century renovations to Watsons Bay Baths, the mood and beauty of the enclosure has not greatly altered since my boyhood swims, or since Harry's postwar fishing expeditions. The water is undoubtedly cleaner, the shark nets have been mended, the pumpkin-retrieving waifs have been replaced by selfie-taking tourists, and accessibility ramps have been added to allow people of all abilities to enjoy a swim. But the overriding feeling one takes away from a splash here is that you're swimming *right in the middle of the harbour*. Like Harry and Mick Doyle vulnerably dangling fishing lines from a bobbing dinghy, a freestyle lap or two of the Watsons Bay Baths involves a direct connection with the harbour. The propellers of an approaching ferry can be heard underwater, an encounter with a jellyfish causes shivers, and the fast-moving progress of sail craft on the other side of the enclosure unnerves and excites. It feels like communing with something big and unpredictable, and for this reason, a swim in what would otherwise be a gentle tidal pool feels thrilling.

The story of my other grandfather, George Baker, is also deeply connected to the drama of Sydney Harbour. In the early winter of 1930, George drowned. The stock market of 1929 had not long crashed, ushering in the Great Depression, and George, a wealthy man, had lost a large amount of money.

When George died, his widow Eve was eight months pregnant with her sixth child, my father. Eve died of cancer 14 years later, leaving my father and his older siblings orphaned. The full story of what happened to George remained largely untold.

Family folklore was that George loved the harbour and the spray of the sea and, while standing on the outside deck of a ferry one evening, accidentally fell overboard. He was wearing a heavy overcoat, which, it was said, had dragged him into the cold, inky sea. His body was washed up on 'one of the harbour beaches' two weeks later: the actual beach was never specified, but it's possible it was Watsons Bay.

My father never questioned this version of his father's drowning (at least to me and my brothers). Was George simply unlucky? Was he murdered? Did he commit suicide? These questions came back to me one afternoon at Watsons Bay when I walked the few hundred metres from the swimming enclosure to The Gap.

Facing the open ocean that runs east of the sandstone cliffs of South Head, The Gap is a Sydney landmark notorious for suicides. The first reported suicide here was in 1863 and, tragically, many people have taken their lives since then. More numerous, however, are the actions by police, rescue workers, locals and bystanders that have prevented suicides. In the 1960s, a German shepherd called Rexie would run and bark whenever she sensed an emergency. It was claimed that Rexie saved more than 30 lives, and a plaque near The Gap commemorates her efforts. More recently, a range of measures such as fencing, signage and an emergency phone with 24-hour access to counsellors has led to a great decrease in the number of tragedies at The Gap. Cameras help to keep the area under surveillance and a virtual fence detecting human movement alerts local police of activity on the cliff side of fences. I was moved by large signs all along The Gap that read 'Call a friend. Call your family. Call us.' and 'Hold onto HOPE. There is always HELP.' They spoke not only of intervention but of a growing awareness in our city of the prevalence and awful realities of suicide.

We will never know if my grandfather George's drowning occurred accidentally or by his own hand. All I know of him are the few stories that my father's oldest sister told of the man who my father never met. I wonder what sort of life he might have lived if he had not drowned in middle age. Given his reported love of the sea, would he have sailed on the harbour, or swum or fished in Watsons Bay? Would he, like most people, have taken a shine to the amiable Harry, who would become his youngest son's father-in-law and his grandchildren's other granddad? The lives of my two grandfathers represent different versions of life lived in proximity to 20th-century Sydney Harbour. One life was long, humble and lacking in opportunity. But it was hugely filled with the consolations of family, friendships and community. The other life was privileged, but it also appeared deeply troubled – or, at best, unlucky.

15
#SHACK

BURNING PALMS, ROYAL NATIONAL PARK

A spectacular stretch of coastline in the Royal National Park, Burning Palms beach typifies a raw littoral life that once existed in many parts of coastal Sydney. Twenty-eight beach shacks, most dating from the 1930s and clustered on the beach's northern headland, give a snapshot of what life was like for poor city folk who opted for coastal subsistence living over the privations of Depression-era Sydney.

In the 1930s, as the worst of the Depression gripped Sydney, many poor families were unable to pay their rent and were evicted from dark and crowded terrace houses in suburbs like Surry Hills, Newtown, Glebe and Balmain. Some packed the few possessions they had and set up life in coastal squatter camps. While the most famous of these was Happy Valley at La Perouse, similar camps existed in Maroubra, Kurnell, Cronulla and Clontarf. Squatters typically built incredibly basic huts on freehold land. Made from rough wooden slabs, tin and hessian, and with roofs of bark and saplings, these huts were the sorts of makeshift shelters one would expect to see in a daguerreotype of a Gold Rush miners' camp.

Slightly less rustic versions of Sydney's original beach shacks survive at Dobroyd Head, at the entrance of Middle Harbour, and in greater numbers on the beaches of Era, Little Garie and Burning Palms in the Royal National Park. The

National Park shacks were the most isolated: they could only be accessed by boat, or by extremely long walks through rough bush terrain. The shacks reflect the isolation, deprivation and lack of services experienced by their inhabitants. They also speak to their occupants' enormous resilience. There was no sewerage or power. Cooking was done on an open fire, and water was collected, one bucket at a time, from nearby creeks. Living a half-day's walk from the nearest train station, road or shop, the 'shackies' were compelled to live a simple life, eating rabbits, fish, birds and homegrown vegetables.

On the day that I visit Burning Palms, it is poignant to see a man carrying a large bag of groceries as he makes the long walk from Waterfall train station into the Royal National Park. Known to my brother and sister in-law who often visit the National Park, the man sleeps rough in the bushland. He politely declines the offer of a ride from my kind brother, and stoically walks on. Like the evicted urban poor of the 1930s, this man has likely been locked out of affordable housing and has gone to live on the city's bushland fringes.

The shacks at Burning Palms are perhaps Sydney's best examples of the Depression-era squatters' huts. Their interiors have changed little since they were built, and while some now have rainwater tanks and solar panels, others are still lit and warmed by kerosene lamps and metho burners. All the shacks were listed on the New South Wales State Heritage Register in 2012 and cannot be privately bought or sold. They remain the property of the original 'shackies' and can only be handed onto immediate family, who nowadays live very much as their ancestors did during the Depression years.

The shacks remain almost as isolated today as they were 90 years ago. To access them, and the beach, you need to drive some distance into the Royal National Park at Waterfall, travel along the rutted dirt road to the car park at Garawarra Farm and then hike a couple of kilometres down the steep escarpment through coastal rainforest. There's nothing on the beach except golden sand, pristine sea and rock pools. Everything you want to eat or drink needs to be carried in.

Burning Palms might not be the most picturesque beach in the Royal National Park, but the reward you feel when you dive into the water after the journey's exertion and sweat makes it the most satisfying. Today's swim is no different. The waves break cleanly over a sandbar and the water is as clear as I have ever seen on a Sydney beach. To fully enjoy its clarity and sparkling effervescence, I wear goggles as I bodysurf. As each wave breaks over me, layers of water explode into thousands of pale-green bubbles, and individual grains of sand dance as the tide stirs the sandbar.

I'd been coming to Burning Palms for more than 30 years but the last time I visited was almost a decade ago. Coming here always felt like an adventure: the effort required to reach the waves; the beach's evocative name, which made me think of the film *Apocalypse Now*; and the small grove of palms that marks the entrance to the sand all seemed mythic. The beach's fantastic Lost Island feeling was amplified by local stories of the shackies' struggles and of epic tales of surfers who carried their boards through the rainforest to catch the perfect wave. Despite a song celebrating it in the 1980s by the Sydney band Van Gogh's Dream, Burning Palms was, until relatively recently, a well-kept secret, mostly known to bushwalkers, surfers and people in the (Sutherland) Shire.

Today I'm shocked to discover that despite the hot walk down to the beach, the relative isolation and the corrosive wind that blows off the sea, the rainforest track is heaving. Literally hundreds of people scurry over a newly installed, high-quality boardwalk. When did this change happen, and why are so many people now coming to Burning Palms?

I soon learn that Burning Palms is not most of the walkers' final destination. The lovely beach is just a junction to pause for a drink of water or a quick dip as they travel to or from their place of pilgrimage a kilometre or two further down the coast: the Figure Eight Pools.

Located in an otherworldly rock shelf, the Figure Eight Pools are most certainly intriguing. Big enough to hold two or three floating adults, the largest of them is a natural pool with deep rock walls that looks just like the number '8'. It can only be accessed at low tide. At other times, it's obscured by the foam of a wild and spurting sea. Maybe its tidal coquettishness adds to its appeal, but I am baffled as to why, with so many astonishing pools, beaches, rock shelves and cliff walks nearby, this relatively tiny pocket of sea shelf draws a crowd the size of a rock concert. The reason lies in two words: social media.

The Figure Eight Pools are social influencers. Their novelty and social media following have made them a brand name and created a cult-like obsession. The pools are especially novel to Chinese visitors who view the number eight as lucky. Like the watermelon cake at Black Star Pastry in Newtown, the ricotta hotcakes at Bills cafe in Darlinghurst and the Bridestowe lavender farm of Launceston, the once little-known Figure Eight Pools now have an international following thanks to Instagram. The heavy traffic of people who come to take a selfie in or near the pools has led to the complete upgrading of infrastructure in this part of the National Park. It's also indirectly boosted numbers to Burning Palms by about 1000 per cent.

It seems ironic that a remote and beautiful place that was

occupied by the exiled poor and marginalised is now a pit stop for Instagrammers who live in the suburbs from which the shackies were originally evicted. It also seems absurd that in spending so much time and effort to walk through rainforest and pristine coastland, people keep walking without much pause at beautiful Burning Palms, and are then prepared to wait in a conga line for a selfie in the spot deemed most special by an app. Such is the fickleness of social media, and of all of us who follow it. In chasing unique 'bucket lists', we join caravans of people from all over the world who want to do exactly the same thing, and in seeking the extraordinary or wanting to emulate others' sense of it, we forget to linger in places that may be more beautiful but less hyped. #crazy.

16
BARE TRUTHS

LADY BAY BEACH, SYDNEY HARBOUR NATIONAL PARK

For a port city with such splendid weather, wonderful beaches and a general air of permissiveness, one might expect nude bathing to be more prevalent in Sydney. Yet for most of its white history, swimming naked has been prohibited.

For millennia, the Gadigal people swam, fished and camped in the region we now call Sydney. Unlike the British colonisers, the Gadigal had no prohibitions on being naked. Their indifference towards nudity was akin to most traditional societies that have existed in warmer climates. Nudity was commonplace in the lives of the Egyptians, Greeks and Japanese, and taboos towards nudity in Western society largely originated with the Age of Enlightenment. Until the 18th century, it was the norm in Europe to bathe naked in rivers, and bathers were not gender segregated. Prudishness towards public nudity took its strongest hold over Anglo society in Victorian times, when it was deemed shameful and obscene to be publicly naked in Britain and its imperial satellites.

Such was the distaste for the naked (or even partially clothed) body in the 19th century that daytime swimming was officially banned in Sydney Cove in 1833. Enforced to protect public decency, the ban was extended in 1838 to all other towns in New South Wales. Later in the century, clothed ocean swimming was tolerated but it was usually gender segregated, and, until the beginning of the 20th century, swimming was officially restricted to the very early morning hours. In 1907, hundreds of bathers gathered in Coogee, Bondi and Manly to oppose the regulation that bathing men wore a 'sea kilt', or swimming skirt, to protect their modesty. Protesters marched behind a dead seagull on a pole, wearing their sisters' petticoats and mothers' kitchen curtains.

With the removal of this requirement and the introduction of all-day bathing, Sydney swimmers began to get more audacious in their attire. In 1907, Annette Kellerman, Australia's swimming champion and a silent-era movie star, was arrested in the United States for wearing a one-piece costume that revealed her legs. Kellerman's notorious arrest helped to challenge censorious attitudes to women's swim-wear – and hugely increased her fame. 'Neck-to-knee' costumes were the norm for men and women until World War II, but in 1945, a year before American nuclear testing first took place on Bikini Atoll, two-piece costumes appeared on Sydney beaches. Women started bathing topless in the 1970s and, advancing aquatic permissiveness, in 1976 the state government of Neville Wran legalised nude bathing at a couple of designated Sydney beaches, including Lady Bay.

Also known as Lady Jane Beach, Lady Bay is a tiny but gorgeous little beach with spectacular harbour views. It is wedged between South Head and Camp Cove. My first and very timid swim there was with a friend in the late 1990s. Heeding the 'slip, slop, slap' campaign for skin-cancer prevention, we dutifully lugged a large beach umbrella and bottles of sunscreen down to the beach. Our leathery, naked fellow beachgoers looked on incredulously as we struggled comically to erect the umbrella, stripped off and then painstakingly applied thick layers of sunblock.

My next swim at Lady Bay happens spontaneously today. Tolerantly indulging my research for this book, my friend S permits an impromptu detour to the beach as we are taking a harbourside stroll. Neither a swimmer nor a nudist, S patiently sits fully dressed on a rock as I peel off my clothes, dive in and enjoy the water that has been warmed by the afternoon sun. Donning goggles and submerging myself with a great sense of freedom and sensuousness, I enjoy the harbour's underwater gardens. Close by, a naked twentysomething couple is 'straw-kelling' – collecting plastic straw-like fragments from the bed of the harbour as they snorkel – and we smile to each other as we cross underwater paths.

In the 20 years or so between my first and second swims at Lady Bay, my attitudes towards nude bathing have changed greatly. Having lived in Berlin for several years (where people are prone to spontaneous dips in the city's lakes, and public nudity is unremarkable), I've learned to shed my self-consciousness with my clothes and enjoy the pleasure of an unplanned naked splash. Many of the lakes in Berlin are signposted with the initials 'FKK', which stands for *Freikörperkultur* ('free body culture') and signals that clothing is optional. I have several amusing memories of my visits to FKK swimming spots and the gradual diminishing of my embarrassment about public nudity. The one image I will always remember is that of a graceful, bronzed lady in her late seventies or early eighties, wearing nothing but an elegant white sun bonnet and a pair of matching gloves that protected her fingers from the newsprint of the broadsheet she was reading.

Any doubts that I might have entertained about German indifference to nudity were dispelled by my visits to my local Berlin swimming pool. While showering after swims, a female attendant (fully clothed in white scrubs and Birkenstocks, and wielding a high-pressure hose) would often approach me in the men's shower cubicle with a business-like *Entschuldigung* ('excuse me') and nudge my naked form out of the way so that she could blast the shower's tiles and grouting until they were pristine.

Unlike the prudish Victorians and their transplanted imperial progeny who colonised our city, the Germans (and the Japanese, and the Scandinavians, and the …) can draw distinctions between nakedness and sex, and nudity and morality. The bare truth is that we all spend the first nine months of our lives floating naked in the wombs of our mothers. We joyfully devote time each day to being naked in or under the water in our bathrooms and, like small children, we could retain a natural enjoyment of being naked in the water if we were not taught otherwise.

It's often said that Sydney Harbour is a playground, and today I enjoy a childlike spontaneity as I frolic uninhibited in the warm water, savouring a small dose of pleasure with innocence and pure joy.

17
THE SIREN

TAMARAMA BEACH

Few beaches in Sydney are as beautiful, or as treacherous, as Tamarama.

Viewed from the heights of Tamarama Marine Drive, Tamarama is quite simply spectacular. Its sand is the colour of 24-carat yellow gold; its rolling waves are shades of cyan. There's a good reason why the beach is nicknamed 'Glamarama'. At the foot of one of Sydney's most desired coastal neighbourhoods, Tamarama Beach is peopled by beautiful, young, teak-coloured women in bikinis and surfers with sixpacks and wet golden locks.

Tamarama has a strange history of being a playground. In the late 19th century, the beach was transformed by colonial hucksters who turned it into the Royal Aquarium and Pleasure Grounds. Pier-side attractions such as merry-go-rounds, Punch and Judy shows and shooting galleries complemented a resident seal pond and tanks of catfish. A fire destroyed the aquarium in 1891, and in 1906 a seaside amusement park called Wonderland City took its place. Taking up all the beach, plus the area where Tamarama Park now stands, Wonderland City displayed sad zoo animals, and offered freak shows and fairground rides to the thousands who came through its 70 turnstiles. The perimeter of Wonderland City was enclosed by wire fences, and it became a daily sport for locals to cut their way through the wire so they could swim at the beach.

Wonderland City went bust five years later and a surf lifesaving club was created on the beach's northern headland. At about this time, the cult of the suntan, and the association of the beach with virility and hedonism began to take hold of the Sydney imagination. Nowadays, Tamarama's more popular recreational pursuits are Pilates and martial arts.

Like a siren from Greek mythology, Tamarama is both alluring and deadly. Lured by its beauty and fame, many an unsuspecting bather has been captivated by the beach's waters only to discover that its undertow is vicious – and sometimes lethal. With more rescues per 1000 swimmers than on any other beach in Sydney, Tamarama is the most dangerous patrolled beach in New South Wales. Tragically, the CEO of publishing house Hachette Australia, Matthew Richell, drowned here surfing when he was washed onto the rocky area known as the Twins. Even in smaller swells, its narrow strip of beach and deep waters generate extremely dangerous rips.

The Sirenum Scopuli, the mythical home of the sirens, is a place surrounded by rocks and cliffs. So too is Tamarama Beach, which is bookended by craggy grey and camel-coloured headlands. The northern sandstone headland is striated with toffee-coloured organic patterns, made over thousands of years by the movement of strong swells. The circular patterns remind me of the Western Desert paintings of Papunya. On this hot autumn day, I've taken shelter under the beautiful headland but, like a sailor from Homer's *Odyssey*, I'm seduced by something otherworldly and forgo my better judgement. Despite the clearly posted 'Beach Closed Dangerous Conditions' sign, I wade waist-deep into Tamarama's waters.

I'm not the only fool. About 15 of us have eschewed the signed warnings and the lifesaver on duty seems resigned to our negligence. 'Please just jump in and jump out – no swimming,' he very reasonably implores through a megaphone. I think back to a swim I had some years ago in Sardinia, somewhat closer to the home of the sirens. Excited to see large waves breaking on a Mediterranean beach, I leaped in and caught two or three dumpers into the shoreline before an extremely irate lifeguard, maniacally waving his arms and violently blowing on a whistle, told me that the beach was closed and that I was a *stronzo* (which, depending on your dictionary, means 'piece of shit', 'arsehole' or 'dickhead').

The Italian lifeguard had fair cause to scold me. Beaches are usually closed for good reason, and in many parts of the world, including Sydney, men are far more likely to drown than women. Every year, about 100 people drown in New South Wales and, based on recent data from the Royal Life Saving Society, almost four times as many men drown as women. While some of these deaths are related to drug and alcohol consumption or simple bad luck, others result from overconfidence, ignorance of local conditions and misguided derring-do. Defying the stereotype of the overseas or inland swimmer unfamiliar with Sydney's beaches, most of the city's drowning victims are local. Social media can also be factor in male drownings, when secret swimming spots which are either unpatrolled or unsafe are promoted. The vast majority of coastal drownings result from people being caught in ocean rips.

I asked Professor Rob Brander ('Dr Rip'), beach safety researcher at the University of New South Wales, how rips are formed. 'Rip currents exist as a mechanism to return water that's been carried shoreward by breaking waves back offshore,' he explained. 'If there's no breaking waves, there won't be any rip currents.' Any beach with wave action will have a slightly higher water level on the shoreline than further offshore. Usually, this higher level of water retreats to the sea, but on narrow beaches like Tamarama, the retreating water slips beneath the waves to form a channel, creating an undertow on its way back out. Contrary to popular belief, undertows don't vertically suck people into a watery abyss. Instead, the fast-moving water of a rip pulls swimmers away from where they think they should be. Instinctively, most of us try to swim against the rip, rather than swimming with it, and instead of literally going with the flow and exiting the water further along the shore, we panic and fight against the current. When the rip is strong and our panic is acute, we become overwhelmed, and our exhaustion and fear become bigger dangers than the actual rip.

Talk to any beach-going Sydney swimmer and you'll likely find that they have experienced being caught in a rip. I've twice been caught in a rip and the terror of seeing the shore retreat is as great as the relief that comes when the rip deposits you on terra firma further north or south from where you entered the sea. My favourite literary evocation of experiencing a rip is in the short story 'The Cathedral' from Tim Baker's collection *Out From the Past*. In the story, two brothers contend with both the rip and a hailstorm, and these forces of nature create a truly epic struggle.

Happily, today doesn't provide my third experience of a rip. Heeding the lifesaver's advice, I retreat to shallow water that is barely a metre deep. The water is clear and refreshing but I respect its power and do four quick laps of the beach to maintain this chapter's credibility. My laps are a 'swaddle' (a cross between a swim and a paddle) and I decide that the day's true swimming is best done in the safe confines of the nearby Bronte ocean baths. I console myself with a coffee on the beautiful deck of the Tamarama cafe.

From the cafe, I can again admire the beach's good looks, and once again I'm smitten. Tamarama is the end point of Sculpture by the Sea, the largest free public sculpture exhibition in the world. During the two-week outdoor arts event, Tamarama's sands are the plinth for many of its most intriguing oversized sculptures. A few years ago, king tides washed away some of the sculptures, including a cage-like installation made of razor wire that contained five rusting human figures. Titled *Fair Dinkum Offshore Processing*, the work by Bronek Kozka drew attention to the traumas and limbo suffered by offshore asylum seekers. The sculpture was violently dragged out to sea and smashed against the craggy rocks that enclose the beach. Literally victims of the rip, all five figures were poignantly lost at sea.

18
DAWN IN APRIL
DAWN FRASER BATHS, BALMAIN

It's not quite 7 am at Dawn Fraser Baths in Balmain and it's April Fools' Day. I'm feeling like the day's namesake because I've left home in the dark, hopped on a train and a bus to meet my friend K, and arrived to discover a dark and closed pool entrance. It's the end of the swimming season here and still daylight-saving time, so dawn has yet to fully arrive. Knowing more than K and I do (and likely having had the luxury of some breakfast), the friendly attendant won't turn up for another 15 minutes. K, who believes that swimming, like most things in life, is best done without fuss and early in the morning, decided that we had to be the first in the water, so here we are.

K is ten years my senior, but made of far tougher stuff than I am. She learned to swim in the cold-water beaches of Victoria, and is a veteran harbour and ocean swimmer. Over the summer, she does a succession of ocean swims that are sometimes several kilometres long.

The pool opens and we are indeed the first to get to the water. As I struggle to make sense of why we're swimming in these first dull daylight hours, K quickly peels down to her one-piece and briskly dives into the water with good-natured gusto and an ear-to-ear grin. Teased by K for dawdling, I eventually join her in the water. The flotsam of leaves, a stray jellyfish and the cool tingle of the salt remind me that this is Sydney Harbour, not a tamed and chlorinated municipal pool. In the early light, the water is a grey jade, and only fuzzy suggestions of life and movement can be seen below its surface.

'The Dawny', a tidal pool situated below Elkington Park on the western side of the Balmain peninsula, is Australia's oldest existing public swimming pool. Predating the venerable Bronte Baths and McIver's Ladies Baths in Coogee, the Dawny was built in 1882 and boasts Australia's oldest swimming and water polo clubs. The heritage pool is listed on the National Trust and on the Register of the National Estate.

Its enclosed timber decking and boardwalks, and two-storey viewing pavilion, are entirely unique. Crazily, the pavilion turns its back on one of the city's best harbour views and is oriented towards the swimming lanes, rather than to Cockatoo Island. When the pool was built, this stretch of the harbour was buzzing with steamships, coal loaders and shipyards so, as well as providing a viewing area, the pavilion was likely designed as a buffer between the recreation of the baths and the industrial activity of the harbour. The first iteration of the pool was completely roofed to protect the modesty of those swimming, but thankfully that disappeared in 1900. Today's pool is essentially the grander version that was built in 1926.

The harbour nowadays is significantly cleaner and more relaxed than it was in Victorian times, and once a year, a community swim takes place from the Dawny to Cockatoo Island and back. K's love affair with harbour swimming began with this swim; when I press her for details, she laconically talks of the egg-and-bacon roll she enjoyed after the swim, rather than describing the effort required to traverse the harbour.

Dawn Fraser, who the Baths were renamed after in 1964, learned to swim here as a young girl in the 1940s. An Olympic legend, Fraser was the youngest of eight children. Local folklore has it that she used to sneak into baths because she couldn't afford the entrance fees. She was spotted swimming by a local swim coach, who persuaded her to swim competitively. Her grit and no-nonsense demeanour were typical of the working-class people who characterised Balmain in the early and mid-20th century.

At about the time that my friend K was first dipping her toes in the water, Fraser became an international sensation at the 1956 Melbourne Olympics. The first of only four swimmers in Olympic history to win a gold medal for the same event at three different Games, Fraser defended her Melbourne 100 metre freestyle victory at the 1960 Rome and 1964 Tokyo Games. During her Olympic reign, she faced some profound personal challenges, losing both her parents within a few years of each other. I think about the parallels with K, who also lost both parents as a young person. K, like Fraser, was steered positively by older siblings, and she too maintained an incredible sense of purpose. K sincerely holds the modest belief that a good life depends on hard work and good luck.

Fraser was often portrayed as a larrikin, and her life out of the pool helped to feed this persona. Soon after her success in the Olympic pool at Tokyo, she notoriously climbed a pole in front of the Japanese emperor's palace to steal a flag. She was subsequently arrested but charges were never laid, and the Japanese police later presented her with the flag and a box of flowers. Fraser, however, was suspended from representative swimming by the Australian Swimming Union and her Olympic career came to an end. In later years, she ran a pub in Balmain, represented Balmain as an independent member of NSW Parliament, and played a significant role as mentor and elder at the 2000 Sydney Olympics.

Like its namesake, the Dawny is venerable and locally beloved. It has also had to fight for its survival. Lashed by king tides in 2018, which inundated some of its facilities, the aging pool was showing critical signs of disrepair. Locals feared that the funds required to urgently renovate the pool and future-proof it against rising sea levels would never be raised, and that, profoundly neglected, this remarkable piece of harbourside real estate would ultimately be demolished. Happily, various tiers of government found the funds to repair and upgrade the pool, and the Dawny received a new lease on life.

Swimming in the Dawny at dawn requires some mettle and a belief that one will feel better for the challenge involved. As Fraser and as K have demonstrated in their not-always-easy and sometimes unconventional lives, struggle can be rewarded with success, and self-belief is fuel for motivation. When life is embraced like a determined dive into the sea at dawn, surprising things can be achieved.

19

THE SACRED AND THE PROFANE

NORTH CURL CURL ROCK POOL

Curl Curl is a place of duality. For many locals, its double-barrelled name is synonymous with pleasure and wellbeing, but several drownings have occurred here, and Curl Curl is regarded as one of Sydney's most dangerous beaches. The North Curl Curl Rock Pool sits some distance north of the beach's constant rough and infamous rip, but it is not entirely a safe haven. The pool is both sheltered from the wind by a dimpled golden headland, and nakedly exposed to the churning surf that intermittently crashes over its boundaries. Bordered by rock shelf on one side and by cement walls on the other, it is half natural and half human-made. It has two rock monoliths that nestle together in the middle of the pool, like surfacing whales, and for me, particularly in the week around Easter, the rock pool is a place of the sacred and the profane.

There is something primordial about this pool. It may be because it is not only physically isolated from car parks and easy access, but also removed from the long stretch of Curl Curl Beach, which itself is surrounded by parks, sand dunes and sea cliffs. The pool can be only accessed from the beach at low tide, and even then, this involves walking through ankle-deep water and agilely scampering over slippery moss-covered rocks. At other times, the pool must be approached from a steep staircase that leads down from a towering headland to the north.

An ancient natural rock shelf forms one side of the pool, which sits on a sandstone platform, making the pool feel as if it is of the rock, rather than built with rock. The sense of the pool rising out of the area's topography is deepened by the two large monoliths that are half-submerged in the middle. Swimming cautiously around them, I feel like I am in a sacred place and that they are sleeping guardians who should be shown respect. In the early 1900s, a natural rock pool was present in the rock platform here and this became the template for the later, larger human-built pool. Between the pool and Curl Curl Beach sit a series of weathered, pockmarked, biscuit-coloured cliffs that harbour caves and mysteries. In his novel *Taboo*, Noongar author Kim Scott suggests that the 3/4 beat of First Nations coastal songs in south-west Australia mirror the sounds of the sea churning against granite. Hearing waves pound against rock, I marvel at the prospect of other possible songs that are literally inspired by nature. Sheltered from the wind and unaffected by the intrusions of contemporary city life, the pool, for most of the year, feels timeless and elemental.

The venerable pool's isolation and sense of serenity disappear over the holidays. Like the waves that fill and refresh the pool and then recede, a human tide of colourful boardies and bikinis, rashies and beach towels, noodles and plastic buckets washes into the pool on this Easter Sunday afternoon. But the pool, a generous 32 by 20 metres, is big enough to accommodate today's larger-than-usual crowds without too much angst, and the pool's communion with the tides means that it doesn't become fetid like an overused council pool.

Hyper from the excitement of eating chocolate Easter eggs for breakfast, kids splash and laugh, transforming the stony pool from a place of contemplation to an aquatic pleasure ground. They straddle the monoliths (don't wake the guardians!), unearth the sand and pebbles on the pool's surface, and look for sea creatures as they paddle, dive and play. Teenagers flirt and dare and play music, eyeing each other with an incipient sexuality, and parents, relishing a four-day weekend, lie around the pool's perimeter in a near-comatose state. For some, church services have been a part of the weekend, but for others the rock pool has been the holiday's primary place of worship as they surrender themselves to the profane.

My own commitment to serious swimming has been binned with the Easter-egg wrappers, and today I'm happy to simply frolic and float. As I recline fully into the gorgeously warm April water that swashes around my ears, I muse on how wonderful it is to surrender to the sensuous. This is so much better than the other great profane Sydney ritual of this particular holiday – going to the Royal Easter Show – though if I found an adult-sized Pixie Bubble or a set of floaties in a show bag, I'd don them immediately with glee.

Alternating between dozes on the warm rocks and lazy, half-hearted strokes along the edges, I realise that I have been enjoying the pool for hours, literally. The pads of my fingers are as wrinkled as if I've soaked in a regal bathtub, and I feel a patina of salt on my body. I read recently that the dimpling of our fingers after sustained contact with the sea is an evolutionary adaptation that allowed coastal and riverine people to catch fish. I don't know if this is true, but I especially like this idea as I recall delicious fish dinners.

As my mind turns back to Easter, I think about the equinox that the pagan/Christian festival celebrates. Weirdly inverted here in Australia, our Easter, which is meant to celebrate the coming of new life and longer days, occurs at a time when days are perceptibly shorter, we are more prone to introspection, and our vegetation is waning. Rather than thinking of bunnies and new blooms and hatching chickens, let's imbue this dramatic time of the year with some local knowledge. Ocean temperatures are still warm, but there are fewer yellowfin bream, garfish and mullet in the water. The lilly pilly is in berry and its waxy fruit tempts rainbow lorikeets and flying foxes, who squawk and befoul our washing and patios, staining everything magenta with their excrement. This is the season when we can soak with relaxed and smiling brethren in a crystal-clear pool that has been sculpted by the wind and sea. This is the season when we can partake in something approaching the sacred.

20
THE CHILDREN
MERMAID BATHS, NORTH BONDI

I'm on my way to the Mermaid Baths at Bondi, and as my bus snakes up Oxford Street and through Bondi Junction, I read about an upcoming Fridays For Future global climate strike. Fridays For Future is a network of children around the world who are building on the legacy of Greta Thunberg and demanding urgent action on the climate crisis. It's an unseasonably warm day, and while the higher-than-average April temperature is great swimming weather, the month's reluctance to ebb to milder weather is unnerving.

The Mermaid Baths are at the far north end of Bondi Beach. The baths are a built tidal enclosure intended for babies and toddlers who are not quite ready for the waves and surf. For many Sydney children, the baths are their first experience of the Pacific Ocean. They are a delightful place to linger. Bubs gurgle and giggle as they bury their toes in the sand, gleefully splash, and paddle or crawl in the clean ocean water with their parents. Between the baths and the grassy knoll to the north, a charming and vibrant mural of aqua fauna created by artist George Rose runs the length of the pool.

Channelling my inner bub, I wade into the baths, plonk down and enjoy the view out to the horizon. With legs stretched out in front of me on the sandy bottom of the pool, the water comes up to my belly button. I circle my toes, make patterns in the water with my hands and enjoy the sploshes and ripples that result from my efforts. It's hardly a swim, but it's delightful. A couple of other adults who are here with their toddlers are doing likewise, and we exchange a smile and acknowledge our shared amusement.

I'm touched by the poise of the little children in the pool and by their innate curiosity and sense of wonder. One little girl, her abundant curls contained by a huge floppy sunhat, squats effortlessly by the water's edge and seems engrossed by the patterns of the light in the water. A little boy in an octopus-patterned rash top submerges a plastic turtle into the water and squeals with joy as it bounces back up to the surface.

I'm also touched by the fragility of this venue. A marker next to the Mermaid Baths was installed by Waverley Council in 2007. Using the results from a CSIRO study into the effect of climate change on rising sea levels, the marker predicted that much of the children's pool would be underwater by 2030. The marker also indicated the projected water height at this point in 2100 and predicted that once these levels occur, Bondi Beach, as well as nearby Tamarama and Bronte, would be inundated. Speaking at the installation of the marker, Waverley's former mayor, George Newhouse, said, 'Our children are our future and we are mortgaging their future by failing to act on this climate change issue.'

The 2007 projections of sea levels used for the Mermaid Baths marker have since been called conservative. According to OzCoasts, a government-funded online database that gives comprehensive information about Australia's coasts based on the research of more than 100 government agencies and universities, the 2007 projection of an 0.88-metre rise in sea levels is a moderate scenario. Coastal Risk Australia have prepared frighteningly vivid interactive maps that depict the consequences of sea-level rises for the year 2100. These scenarios have been combined with a nominal highest astronomical tide and, shockingly, show that much of coastal and harbourside Sydney will be underwater.

The Coastal Risk maps don't take account of possible mitigation measures such as the building of new seawalls, but neither can they consider the impact of storm surges and erosion, which have increased in past years. In just the last few years, storm surges, extreme tidal activity and several 'once-in-a-century' weather events have closed access to beaches at Collaroy, Balmain, Nielsen Park, Garie and Werrong, and necessitated huge unanticipated investment in coastal infrastructure. Sydney's beloved ocean pools – fragile because of their age, construction materials and location – are particularly vulnerable. It's been estimated that natural disasters induced by climate change could cost New South Wales $9 billion a year by 2060.

Mira is 14 and studying marine science, and like many young Sydneysiders and their global peers in the Fridays For Future movement, she is becoming increasingly frustrated with inaction on climate change. I ask why climate change is such an important issue for young people. 'The older generation did nothing,' she says, 'and if we don't do something, we're just going to leave it to the next generation.' Mira's worries echo the projections of the Coastal Risk maps. 'Rising temperatures mean higher sea levels, bigger waves, more erosion, more wave action, floods, disasters, and more animals dying. The bigger waves will eat away at the coastline, and there'll be no beaches left.'

Many of the kids who paddle in the Mermaid Baths go on to join the Bondi Nippers, part of the fantastic 'surf ed'

Nippers program that teaches kids from 5 to 13 years of age about surf awareness and safety. Wearing bright-pink rashies, they are a joy to watch on a Sunday morning as they sprint into the surf, hold hands against the tide, swim through plastic hoops and paddle on their little boards. While the focus of Nippers is squarely on having fun, the program also teaches kids to be safe in the water and to look after each other. The Nippers share a love of the surf, a concern for each other and a healthy respect for the vagaries of ocean. How heartbreaking to think that without action to mitigate the rising of sea levels, the grandchildren of today's bubs, Nippers and Fridays For Future teenagers will have no Bondi Beach to play on.

21
THE PEN IS MIGHTIER THAN THE BOARD
THIRROUL POOL

I've woken early in Thirroul, a little coastal town just south of the limits of metropolitan Sydney, and the day's first light is hitting the silver ocean. Making the most of the unusual luxury of a swim before breakfast, I immediately accept an invitation from one of the friends who are hosting me to accompany him to Thirroul Pool. It's an overcast weekday morning and we share the pool with a couple of chatty senior locals and a kids' swim squad.

Insanely separated from a glorious ocean view by a high brick wall, the pool is fed by jadeite-green salt water pumped directly from the ocean. Local folklore tells that a young girl jumped into the pool as it was being emptied. She was sucked through the gurgling outlet pipe before being deposited on the sand at the end of the pipe, amazingly uninjured. As compensation for the madness of obscuring the beach views, the pool charges no entry fee and offers views of grand Norfolk Island pines and the Illawarra Escarpment.

As we swim enough laps to summon a sense of endorphin-rich wellbeing, I begin to appreciate the pool's lovely details. Its deep end is 2.6 metres and there's a drama to looking some way down to the bottom, especially because it's dusted in sand and strewn artfully with kelp. At the shallow end, I'm struck by the period tile work – yellow and black tiles look like piano keys, and 1940s red terracotta tiles that trim the pool's perimeter and cover its steps add a jazzy contrast. There's a love to both the construction and the locals' use of the pool, and I find myself reaching for words to do this justice.

I've been in Thirroul two days and words have been a key feature of my getaway, since the couple who are hosting me are both talented writers. As I snooze, or read, or swim, or cogitate, they write with a daily discipline and effort that distinguishes the professional wordsmith from the dozing dilettante. Instead of writing like my companions, I find myself wandering Thirroul Beach, looking at the blue horizon from their balcony and thinking about people who are compelled to write about the sea.

Tragic tales loom large in Thirroul. The brig *Amy* was wrecked on Thirroul Beach in 1898 and none of its crew of eight survived. A memorial to the lost sailors near the beach reads: 'O hear us when we cry to thee, for those in peril on the sea.' This inscription might also memorialise Brett Whiteley, one of Australia's greatest artists, who died from a heroin overdose in a Thirroul motel room in 1992. In the 1970s, Whiteley had made a number of drawings of the sea, which are simple and joyful; while drawing them, he had spoken of 'an expandingness' that emanated from the waves. Poignantly, his last sense of life may have been the sound of crashing surf.

Thirroul's dramas and its wild coastline are the stuff of great writing, and one name often associated with Thirroul is that of a writer: DH Lawrence. The English novelist and his wife Frieda arrived here in 1922 and rented a cottage called Wyewurk, which overlooked the ocean not far from Sandon Point, half an hour's walk from Thirroul Pool. Lawrence inverted the pun of the house's name and over a winter wrote furiously, famously producing most of the novel *Kangaroo*. Thirroul features largely in the novel but Lawrence renamed it 'Mullumbimby', perhaps to sound more 'Australian' for an English readership.

While he chose not to interact with the Thirroul community and thought the town was 'strange and forlorn', Lawrence alternately describes the Pacific as 'quiet as a purring cat with white paws', 'rhythmic' and 'thunderous'. He was hugely inspired by the sound and power of the ocean, which at times was so loud that it made indoor conversations difficult to hear. Lawrence loved Thirroul's rock pools at low tide. He marvelled at how they filled with clear water and teemed with crimson anemones. He was also transfixed by the bushland dividing the ocean from the escarpment, describing it at night as 'raving with moonlight'.

Australian writer Ashley Hay located her 2013 novel *The Railwayman's Wife* in 1940s Thirroul. One of its characters carries a copy of *Kangaroo* 'like a literary Baedeker' or guidebook, and wanders the town hoping to find identifiable spots and recognisable people that align with Lawrence's fiction. Lawrence, the beach, writing and books figure greatly in Hay's novel, and she describes the Railway Institute Library, which used trains to transport books to railway workers. Like the Illawarra ocean pools that were built to nurture the bodies of coal workers, the Railway Institute Library sought to nourish workers' minds.

DH Lawrence wasn't the first visiting writer to be moved by Sydney's waters. Before his visit to Sydney, Mark Twain, Joseph Conrad and Arthur Conan Doyle wrote about the city's coastlines. The Sydney Writers Walk at Circular Quay celebrates some of these writers' quotes. More recently, at the Sydney Writers' Festival, British writer David Mitchell told the audience how inspired he was by Sydney Harbour and described it as a great blue 'unironed sheet'.

Given we are the world's largest island, it's no surprise that many of Australia's most celebrated writers have felt compelled to write about the sea. Tim Winton's descriptions of his home state have vividly brought the Western Australian coastline into the imagination of eastern-state and international readers. Robert Drewe's short stories and Peter Corris's novels situate contemporary Australian drama by or on the beach, and Louis Nowra beautifully describes the water of Sydney Harbour as 'one great act of affirmation, an open heart that invites you to take Sydney personally'.

In *The Railwayman's Wife*, words are transformative, and so is the power of the sea. After my swim this morning, I better realise the capacity of one to inform the other. As we towel off, ideas start to ripple. We grab a coffee at the Art Deco cafe next door and, looking at the morning sun break through clouds onto the waves, I actually gasp. For the first time since I've been in Thirroul, I suddenly need to write about the sea.

22
PUBERTY BLUES
GUNNAMATTA BAY BATHS, CRONULLA

To long-time residents of the (Sutherland) Shire, Cronulla is the jewel in the crown of the Godzone (or 'God's Own Country'). Locals, including former prime minister Scott Morrison, speak proudly of Cronulla's strong sense of community. This is exemplified by friendly dog walkers, a large number of well-attended sporting clubs, and the huge amount of money raised by the suburb's volunteers for the Cancer Council's annual Relay For Life events. The hardy men and women who swim year-round at Gunnamatta Bay Baths are also a celebrated part of the area's community spirit.

Gunnamatta Bay is part of the Port Hacking estuary, and the suburbs of Cronulla, Woolooware and Burraneer sit on the bay's east, north and west respectively. It's a five-minute walk from Cronulla railway station, and a cute little wooden ferry that looks like a child's bath toy plies the waters between Gunnamatta and Bundeena in the Royal National Park.

This part of the Shire was my world for the last two years of my school education. When I was 16, my family moved from Campsie to Blakehurst. After finishing Year 10 at a multicultural boys' school in Marrickville, I enrolled in a Catholic, co-ed senior school in monocultural Cronulla and experienced the first of many life instances of culture shock. It was the early 1980s and the Cronulla I encountered at school was not too different to the one evoked in Kathy Lette and Gabrielle Carey's novel *Puberty Blues.*

Cronulla for a teenager in the 1980s was about getting wasted and fitting in. I remember being stunned by the binge drinking that occurred at the first school party that I went to as a not-quite-17-year-old. Surfer boys threw back beer from longneck bottles, surfer girls drank 'goon' – cheap cask wine – and everyone smoked like chimneys. Not able to discern whether I was hugely attracted or hugely repelled, I recall watching a strapping schoolboy footballer quickly get hammered and then rip lemons from a backyard tree, which he cockily threw at the most vulnerable-looking guests. Before a party began, bongs were smoked in the back of panel vans parked in suburban cul-de-sacs or beachside car parks. The bongs were ingenious affairs, made from Orchy orange juice containers and plastic tubing that was cut from residents' garden hoses. If not trashed at a backyard party, the school's kids spent weekend evenings sweatily bouncing to bands like Australian Crawl, INXS, Men at Work and Mental as Anything, who regularly played at local pubs. Bouncers were largely indifferent to obviously underage patrons, and on many an evening kids on P-plates drove home drunk or stoned.

Our school sat on the edge of Gunnamatta Bay, and its first-floor classrooms looked onto its shimmering waters. One of our classmates who lived in Bundeena came to school each day in a dinghy, which he tied at the end of a pier just beneath the school's grounds. As a child who'd grown up in landlocked south-west Sydney, I found this extraordinary. Kookaburras and cockatoos sometimes watched over the playground, which was fringed with grand eucalypts. Unlike the hedonism of weekends, school days were disciplined and regulated. Boys expressed rebellion by wearing their shirt tails out, and girls with more than one earring in an ear were reproached. We learned about Ancient Greece and the Cold War, but little mention was made of Indigenous Australia; a handful of students studied foreign languages, and a highlight of the year for the biology students was the dissection of a frog. Teachers tried to befriend or berate us, and a local priest came to the school once a term to remind us to 'just say no' when sex reared its troubling head.

While I loved the after-dark live music scene of the Shire in the 1980s, I didn't fit into the school's surfer culture or any of its many sporty tribes. As if speaking a foreign language, the surfie boys talked of 'sets' and 'grommets' and 'scungies', and the closest I ever came to being a high school sportsman was playing table tennis at lunchtime. As a young boy, I had sometimes come with my family to swim at South Cronulla Beach, but I was now informed by kids at school that this was where the 'westies and wogs' swam. Feeling like a fish out of Cronulla water, I sought out other non-local misfits with world views that were more akin to mine: a Spanish boy, an English boy, a German boy, a Dutch boy. One of my friends was a boy whose family was Calabrian. His hobby and party trick was to make small explosive devices. He'd spend days patiently filling soda siphon gas bulbs with iron filings and then, on a Friday evening, he'd gleefully use these to decimate the letterboxes of large suburban houses. I also forged friendly alliances with some girls who'd grown up in different parts of Sydney, and who, like me, enjoyed movies, books, drama, debating and skipping.

Once I left school, I gave Cronulla short shrift, going to university, moving into the inner city, and then living overseas for many years. My return visits to Cronulla started about 15 years ago when I regularly took my mother, who was widowed and living at a care home in the Shire, to the rock pools for a swim. After Mum died, I continued to visit her best friend, an effusive, big-hearted character who lived in Cronulla, and each time I visited I stole a swim at a rock pool.

Every time I get off at Cronulla Station, I have a strange mix of feelings. It's a bit like going back to a family home as an adult and sleeping in a childhood bedroom. In some ways, it's familiar and very comforting. I think with a smile of the energy, naivety and friendships of my adolescence. And then a ripple of contrasting emotion counters the nostalgia as I recall the less-than-stellar feelings of being a self-censoring and repressed gay boy in a Catholic school in which teachers, peers and the community exalted a culture of straight, monocultural, masculine muscularity. It's not fair to say the Shire wasn't a welcoming place – it was, and it is. People are kind and gregarious and generous, and they happily banter. But being different, I always felt the Shire had a mild suspicion of anyone who didn't conform.

It's been years since I've swum at Gunnamatta Bay – the last time might have been just after I finished my Higher School Certificate exams. It's a mid-autumn afternoon and, thinking that the sheltered westerly aspect of Gunnamatta might be more pleasant than the breezy east-facing coast, I turn right rather than left from the train station. I walk past the possum-occupied, giant grey gums and the picnic pavilions of Gunnamatta Park and come to the bay's swimming enclosure. At more than 180 metres long, the enclosure gives swimmers more than enough room to stretch and cut loose. An elevated wharf extends at right angles from the beach out to the furthest end of the enclosure. It's a popular place for fishing, and because the green water below is always deep, it's also favoured as a great spot to bomb. It's a weekday and I'm surprised to see a couple of teenage boys bombing with abandon. I wonder whether they're jigging from my old school, which I can now see from the top of the wharf. The boys egg each other on and laugh throatily as they leap off the wharf. I can't help but smile at their bravado and obvious enjoyment, but a couple of older men who are fishing nearby seem irritated by the ruckus.

I'm in no hurry, so I let the boys bomb away without intruding into their domain. The midday sun is warm, and I peel off my clothes and lie on the wooden planks of the wharf. A visit to a dermatologist had brought me to the Shire earlier today, and getting an 'all clear' from the skin doctor, I indulge in a bit of autumnal sunbathing in the same way that I treat myself to something sweet after I see my dentist. After about 10 minutes, I've had a good dose of vitamin D without getting burned and, conveniently, the boys have exhausted their arsenal of bombs. Still laughing, they run down the wharf.

A 50-metre lap pool is embedded within the main enclosure, and having the pool to myself, I decide it's now time to climb down a 2-metre ladder that leads from the wharf to a wooden pontoon at the south end of the lap pool. I dive off the pontoon and swim the pool's length several times. The wharf is supported on four corners by concrete pylons, and swimming in the lap pool feels like swimming under a bridge. Oddly, the enclosure makes me feel separated from the beauty of the bay, rather than embraced by it.

The water is beer-bottle green, and I feel like I am encased and moving within an emerald cube. No marine life, no plants or weed, and no flotsam greet me. Today, this beautiful bay feels strangely sterile. Swimming in the opaque water feels like returning to puberty: I feel entirely self-absorbed, and there is no reference point to anything other than myself. The only indicators of a world existing beyond this monotone aquatic environment are the sound of my breathing and the white foam caused by my strokes.

Without the distractions of shoreline views or under-water life, I fall into a deeply reflective state. Maybe the glimpse of my old school from the wharf and the sight of two teenage boys bombing wilfully has disturbed memories of my adolescence that were, till now, happily lying dormant. Things I haven't thought of for many years surface with each breath and stroke. My 17-year-old self is swimming with me today, and I feel like it's important to be kind to him. As I swim, I tell him that places and people and attitudes change, and that, as boys become men, feelings of difference can lead to precious and life-sustaining relationships.

I climb out of the green water, surprised by the intensity of the emotions of my swim, and by the evanescence of these feelings as I clamber up the ladder and back to the wharf. My 17-year-old self, it seems, has stayed in the water. Looking back to my old school now feels like looking at an artefact in a museum display case. It's of mild interest but is no longer emotionally arresting. I turn towards the beach and walk along the wharf with my back to the school, leaving behind the memories that surfaced.

23
EXILE AND QUARANTINE
LITTLE BAY BEACH

It is astonishing that in a city of five million people, you can hop on a weekday bus and, within half an hour of leaving Central, be on a beach that is almost entirely empty. Little Bay is one of Sydney's least visited beaches. It's also one of the city's calmest and loveliest for swimming. Other than a fisherman, a local resident walking her dog, and a buffed and tanned male model doing a swimwear photo shoot with a photographer, my friend R and I have the bay to ourselves on this windless, sunny mid-week day.

The furthest south of Sydney's 'eastern' beaches before you get to Botany Bay, Little Bay is a remarkably beautiful spot. It consists of three small sandy beaches framed by a rocky headland at one end and a golf club that occupies a spot that was once a quarantine facility at the other. A surf break a couple of hundred metres out from the beaches ensures that the bay's water is calm, without a rip and ideal for ocean swimming.

As we swim towards the break on a clear May morning, my sense of elation grows with each stroke. Treading water, R and I watch the surf break on the reef, and laugh at our good fortune and the bracing beauty of the day.

There is something incredibly remote about Little Bay, and this is accentuated by the absence of others and the remnants of the area's history. In the 19th century, the Dharawal

110

people who had long lived here were forced to move to other areas, such as La Perouse, when Little Bay became a smallpox isolation camp. Its history of quarantine continued with the building of the Coast Hospital in 1881, which housed victims of Sydney's 1900 outbreak of bubonic plague, and many of the soldiers from World War I who returned home suffering from the catastrophic Spanish flu pandemic. Seventy years later, a wing of Prince Henry Hospital, built on the site of the Coast Hospital, was used to segregate those suffering from the AIDS epidemic from the wider community. Even the nurses who tended the sick were isolated at Little Bay: a tiny bogey hole was built on the bay's southern shelf to separate swimming nurses from the sharks that visited the area.

My first memories of Little Bay are of sickness and isolation. As a teenage boy, I went to Prince Henry Hospital to visit a family friend who had suffered an aneurysm. Put into a World War II–era ward, our friend lay in a darkness and silence that was hoped would be neurologically recuperative. My associations of gravitas and tragedy with Little Bay were reinforced many years later when I drove into one of the area's apartment complexes to pick up people and take them to a funeral at the nearby Eastern Suburbs Crematorium. We were mourning a dear friend who'd died long before her time of a brain haemorrhage.

Little Bay always struck me as somewhere at the 'end of the line', and until the 1960s, it was literally this for Sydney's south-east tram network. Apart from its use as a precinct of quarantine, the area was also a dumping ground for Sydney's primary sewage at the nearby Malabar cliff-face outfalls. Until the 1990s, raw sewage spilled into the water, turning the ocean brown and staining the rocks and headlands. Beach historian Caroline Ford documents how these sewage slicks infected bathers at Little Bay and environs with ringworm, 'surfer's foot', typhoid, and countless ear, nose, throat, chest, skin, bowel, liver and eye infections. The construction of a new sewage plant at Malabar in the 1990s greatly reduced these problems, but the area remained 'stained' by its reputation, and to many Sydneysiders was long considered a no-go area. Little Bay's notoriety was perhaps further compounded by its proximity to Long Bay gaol, and by the tragic and freakish attack on a scuba instructor by a great white shark.

The perception of Little Bay as the last outpost of Sydney's civilisation might have contributed to its choice as the site for Christo and Jeanne-Claude's extraordinary art installation *Wrapped Coast – One Million Square Feet*. Wrapping almost two and a half kilometres of the bay's northern headland in white fabric and rope, the two artists, assisted by an army of Australian artists and student volunteers, created the world's largest artwork in 1969. It was so big that there was no vantage point from which the entire work could be viewed. Photos of the installation are quite simply incredible. The shrouded headland looks like a landscape one might encounter in glacial Iceland or on an interstellar parallel world. Hugely controversial, the artwork gave two emerging artists their first international acclaim and sharply divided local sensibilities. It was the first work in almost six decades of incredible Kaldor Public Art Projects, and Christo and Jeanne-Claude went on to wrap Paris's Pont Neuf and Berlin's Reichstag.

Unwrapped, unstained by effluent, and unpopulated by the sick or shunned, the headlands of Little Bay still exude a mystery and a sense of quarantined calm. The Sydney housing boom has ensured that this coastal location is no longer forgotten. Prince Henry Hospital has been redeveloped and much of its grounds now host high-end apartments. Yet the new residential buildings are low-rise, and the headlands' contours hide them from the water's edge. As we emerge from our May swim with our backs to the surf break, a feeling of introspection lodges in me. Except for a plane climbing into the sky, all traces of modern Sydney seem to have disappeared. I leave this site of isolation and recuperation, and for the rest of the day I remain in a state of quiet reflection.

24
OUR POOL

MACCALLUM POOL, CREMORNE POINT

Sydney is a city that has long been divided by postcodes. Asking someone 'Where do you live?' is often code for 'What social class or tribe do you belong to?' Usually within a few seconds of someone's answer, assumptions are made about income, education, social status, race, sexuality and political affiliations. For Sydneysiders, the east/west and north/south divides have long fed notions of identity, rivalry and aspiration. One of the most historically persistent psychological divides in Sydney is the rift between the south and north shores of the harbour. I still joke with friends who live north of the Sydney Harbour Bridge that I am 'crossing into the dark side' when I deign to visit them. They usually reply with a rolling of the eyes and a smile of indulgence that connotes pity for someone who will never quite know what he's missing out on.

I'm guilty of many presumptions about life north of the bridge. I think of the Lower North Shore as a place of long-held privilege and exclusion, so I am both delighted and stunned to find that it houses Sydney's most glorious free council swimming pool.

Today is a day of surprises. It's a mild May weekday afternoon a couple of days after a federal Budget. Stepping off a ferry at Cremorne Point, I walk abreast with a former high-ranking federal cabinet minister. I like that he has no minders and that he takes public transport. I feel that given the pleasant weather and the relaxed atmosphere of the ferry crossing from Circular Quay, it would not be too preposterous to strike up a discussion about the Budget as we step off the gangplank together. But then I'm happy that I decide not to engage him and, like the other few passengers that disembark, I ignore that he's an ex-minister and respect his right to simply be a smiling commuter enjoying the sea, the sunshine, and the bob of the pontoon.

Exiting the pier, I'm on Cremorne Point. Three kilometres of the point's foreshore has been set aside as public land, and it's a ravishing place. A mix of native bush and immaculately tended gardens, Cremorne Reserve contrasts other outrageously expensive residential harbour enclaves in that its foreshore is all publicly accessible and it favours pedestrians over cars. Beyond the reserve sit grand English Revival mansions and interwar-era apartment buildings. A few people lie, sit, picnic or work on the public lawns, and it's impossible not to be wowed by the superb 180-degree views of the harbour, the Opera House, Fort Denison and the city skyline.

The Cremorne peninsula and the stretch of harbour that surrounds it has been contested for almost 250 years. After its initial theft from the Cammeraygal people, it was gifted to a squatting Scottish watchmaker and transformed into an English-style pleasure garden. The peninsula's late-19th-century history of activism seems surprisingly contemporary. It was surveyed for mineral exploration and then slated for residential development. Community groups joined forces with the local council to protest imminent industrialisation. They raised concerns about pollution and mining, informed the wider community of its recreational value and beauty, and successfully fought for Cremorne Point's preservation.

Walking west through the reserve, I come to a fork in a path. Its left arm leads down through a canopy of ferns, palms and fig trees towards the waterfront. This is where I first lay eyes on MacCallum Pool. It's hard to not be charmed by this unique heritage pool. Merging 21st-century water safety and Art Deco architectural detail, a heritage-green picket fence with a childproof gate invites the swimmer in. Feeling like I'm popping in to see a neighbour, I see a 33-metre in-ground pool that happens to be on the foreshore and is massaged by the ripples of the harbour.

Unlike many of the other great swimming spots on Sydney Harbour, the pool isn't tidal. It's fed by salt water pumped from the harbour below, but its sky-blue concrete shell sits on a rock shelf and is enclosed by a wooden deck, a picket fence, and a lovingly tended but modest rockery and garden. The pool is drained and cleaned once a week, and with the next cleaning due tomorrow morning, there are patches of algae on the bottom of the pool. A dozen or so footprints can be seen in the green build-up, making me think that a mad game of Twister has just been played. The footprints also add to the intimacy of the pool. There are not enough marks of individual feet stepping into the water to suggest that this place is abuzz with autumn swimmers. While its views are among the most spectacular in Sydney, the pool's general atmosphere is more akin to a backyard pool than a harbourside resort. As well as the child safety gate, there are gentle reminders not to bring glass in.

The pool's 1930s pedigree is clearly seen in little details like the salmon-coloured pump room with its semicircular pediment that bears the pool's name in a Deco font. The pool was restored in keeping with this heritage theme by the local council in the 1980s. The forest-green paint on the fence that separates the deck from the harbour is slightly peeling, and I think of homes owned by elderly people that are greatly loved but in need of a little more attention to maintenance. Thick rope connects green wooden palings on the other side's boardwalk, closest to the pool, and this speaks to the maritime context of MacCallum.

Today, I have the pool to myself. Well, not entirely to myself. While I'm the only swimmer in the water, a couple of backpackers are making out on a corner of the wooden boardwalk. I wonder how they've come to know about this gem of a pool that most of my Sydneysider friends are unaware of.

The water's cold but not numbing, and with my swim cap on, I'm tingling with wellbeing after eight or nine laps. As I swim up and down the length of the pool, I enjoy spying the harbour and the skyline through a gap between the top of the concrete pool and the decking. These million-dollar glimpses, rather than the exertion of my strokes, have me gasping, and I feel like I've climbed over the fence of a mansion and stolen a swim in the pool of a tycoon. I rinse off under the cold-water shower, humming as I look across the harbour to the Opera House.

MacCallum Pool completely challenges my preconceptions about the North Shore, and this is why I love it. Here on the shores of the harbour, in one of the county's most affluent suburbs, is a free neighbourhood pool. This pool is an inversion of the trappings of social privilege. Anyone can come here, anytime. It's not 'Their' Pool, it's Our Pool.

The pool had its origins as a co-op of sorts. It started as a rock pool built by Fred Lane, a local who also happened to be Australia's first Olympic swimming champion. The pool was then reconstructed by Hugh MacCallum, another local, who worked with neighbours to maintain it. Their goal was to proudly care for something special and to make it available to anyone who came. This strikes a strong chord with me. During the past few weeks of pre-Budget speculation and more recent Budget post-mortems, there has been much discussion of fairness and equity, and it's got me thinking about class and egalitarianism in Australia. Called 'the C-word' by Tim Winton, class is often ignored in public discourse, and poverty is still presumed by many to have been erased by decades of continuous economic growth. However, the incomes of the top fifth of the country have outgrown the incomes of those at the bottom by more than six times, and that's left many Australians poor, homeless, ill and socially immobile. Winton speaks of the plight of the 'the cleaners, the carers and hospitality workers … the casuals, [the] women, [the] migrants', who, working in non-unionised jobs or the gig economy, 'have little bargaining power'. Australia's working poor are often overlooked, while the richest members of the country amass greater and greater wealth.

I think of these Australians as I swim in this contradictory place – a free public pool in the shadow of privilege that looks out to the brash affluence of a global city. MacCallum Pool is free to all, but how many of us in this city of five million have the luxury of a weekday swim here?

25
THE SECRET RIVER
BROOKLYN BATHS

An hour away from Central Station lie the well-kept secrets of the Hawkesbury River. As I take the Newcastle train out of Sydney on this late-autumn day, the leafy suburbs of the Upper North Shore are shedding their leaves in a flurry of gold and rust, and the first sprigs of wattle are appearing. They're an indication that this long (perhaps too-long) summer may soon be over, so I feel particularly happy to have stolen today to swim in the twisting and mysterious waters of the Hawkesbury. At Berowra, suburbia gives way to native bushland and undulating sandstone ridges, and traces of the city recede.

Hawkesbury River railway station feels like a different world and it's hard to believe that Central is just 60 kilometres away. Exiting the station, I approach Brooklyn, a sweet hamlet right on the river that is home to about 700 people. It consists of a few late-19th-century timber buildings, some tourist services, a marina, and water-fringed hills where houses hide among bushland and hearty gardens. Before being linked to Sydney by train in 1887, Brooklyn was an isolated oyster-farming and fishing village, and a sense of remoteness from the city lingers today.

On this cloudy day, the sky and water are the colour of the oysters that this river is famous for. The silver river gently ripples, and the plopping sounds of its movement are more defining than its colours or shape. The rhythm of its lapping is occasionally overwhelmed by the outboard motors of small speedboats that come and go from the marina, and the creaking pontoon of a public wharf that sounds like a native bird mimicking a string instrument. Listening to this sonic competition, I think of James Worner's beautiful short story 'An Island Life', in which the Hawkesbury is described with sounds, smells and feelings rather than visual images: it's a place where 'spent two-stroke' (engine oil) greets the day and mornings are 'heavy' and 'clammy', 'like mangrove flats at low tide'.

I walk a few hundred metres to the Brooklyn Baths, which extend out from the southern bank of the Hawkesbury and are enclosed on three sides by a wooden boardwalk. Metal pylons and bars support the boardwalk. They have been built to exclude the sharks that swim upriver into brackish water from Broken Bay, and the barrier is crusted in oyster shells. The tidal waters are often shallow, and a marker tells me today that the baths are less than 2 metres at their deepest point. A little grassy park borders the pool's fourth perimeter, and behind it are a picnic table, a public barbecue, and a breezeblock change room with showers. I have all this public amenity to myself; a brush turkey is my only companion. A pelican suddenly flies directly overhead, its beak pointed purposefully in navigation and its large wings flapping powerfully. I'm more used to seeing these large and wonderful birds fossick and eat than fly; airborne, a few metres above me, the pelican looks like a fighter jet with a beer gut.

I enter the water from a small sandy beach on the baths' south-west corner. A large, beached jellyfish tells me to be vigilant. Encountering these slimy creatures underwater always gives me a hideous shiver. The golden sand turns to dark mud once I cross the river's threshold and my feet squelch as if treading through potter's clay. To avoid an extended Mr Bean moment of sinking deeper with each step, I do a shallow dive and swim out to the edge of the enclosure. The water is invigorating and there's something comforting about its quicksilver shallows. With every stroke, I feel like I'm being embraced by a molten and magical force, and despite some trepidation about meeting another jellyfish, I like that beneath the surface of the water I can see very little, just the movement of grey water flowing around my body.

The last couple of swims I've done this month have brought on a case of post-dip shivers, but today I get out of the water and feel warmer rather than cooler. Maybe it's the illusion of having just bathed in mercury, or maybe the mysteries of the silver river have sufficiently distracted me from feeling cold. I towel off and sit on the grass, looking at the river and its layered, semi-obscured headlands. It's a scene of infinite bush-shrouded peninsulas and inlets. The Hawkesbury begins in the highlands of the Blue Mountains and then, after 120 kilometres of twists and turns and segues, mightily discharges itself into the Pacific. Looking at just a small fraction of its foreshore fringe, I'm enthralled by its scale and by the knowledge that most of its coves and habitats are hidden. In her passionate and magnificent novel, *The Secret River*, Kate Grenville describes the Hawkesbury as a river that reveals itself 'teasingly, never more than a bend at time, calm between its walls of rock and bush'.

The monotone view seems charged today, and it evokes so much of the river's past. If a film was made of the Hawkesbury's history, the view from Brooklyn Baths would make a powerful establishing shot. To the north-west are the twisting tributaries of Mooney Mooney Creek and Mullet

Creek, backed by the shale, sandstone and eucalypts of the Brisbane Water National Park, a repository of significant First Nations cultural sites. Like much of the Hawkesbury, the tributaries of Mooney Mooney emerged more than 10000 years ago with the end of the last Ice Age as rising sea levels advanced further inland. First Nations peoples lived on this country long before the waters rose, and when the new foreshores were created, they adapted to the habitats of higher waters until they were violently displaced by the colonisers.

Today, I can't but muse on the possible historical parallels between imminent rising waters and the flooded inlets of 10000 years ago. As if to make those parallels seem more pressing, a 30-carriage freight train crosses the low railway embankment that leads out of Brooklyn. It's heading south and is loaded with tonnes of coal, likely mined from the Hunter Valley. I wonder if some of this coal, which will one day burn in a power station here or abroad, will somehow, if even infinitesimally, add to a future rise in the river's waters, and if this might inundate the embankment on which the coal train now travels.

Turning my gaze east, I look to Little Wobby Beach. Like its neighbour Dangar Island, Wobby seems a riverside idyll and its residents speak tenderly of its peace and beauty. After the displacement of First Nations people, these areas were mostly the domain of fishing and oyster-farming communities, but now they increasingly house commuters and Sydney sea changers. Beyond Wobby, at the river's mouth, lies Patonga, which was a lucrative oyster-farming area for many decades. In 2013, the little-understood POMS (Pacific Oyster Mortality Syndrome) virus wiped out farms here and scientists believe that POMS may continue to threaten newly resistant breeds of oysters. Spreading quickly, and malevolently destroying large areas of oyster beds, POMS has been likened to a bushfire at sea. The virus appears to occur in seawater with temperatures of 21 to 25 degrees Celsius, so warming oceans may bode very badly for Hawkesbury oyster farmers if this sinister blight is a by-product of global warming.

How we adapt to rising and warming waters might be the ultimate secret that the Hawkesbury holds. Unlike the First Nations people who, over thousands of years, adapted to the river as it took on its unique and mysterious topography, we may find time is against us as we mitigate the impacts of a changing climate. On this increasingly sombre afternoon, the sky has assumed a bilious tint and I feel melancholy as I ponder the challenges that this beautiful river might have to meet. The clouds and western sun have turned the river sepia. Like the rich brown pigment derived from the ink sacs of cuttlefish that is used to colour nostalgic images of a long-gone past, the river seems ethereal and fragile.

26

ON GOLDEN POND

LAKE PARRAMATTA

Spoiled by its huge number of ocean and harbour beaches, Sydney unsurprisingly gives little thought to its lakes. Even the terrific guidebook *Wild Swimming*, which lists 250 swim spots in the greater Sydney area, pays scant attention to the city's lakes. It briefly mentions Lake Narrabeen but entirely omits Lake Parramatta.

I wonder whether lakes generally get a bad rap. If I think of lakes, I unwittingly also think of risk, menace and secrets. My mental associations of lakes with all things sinister might exist because so many of the films and TV series that I've seen set in or around lakes invariably involve foul play and dark acts. In Jane Campion's *Top of the Lake*, a detective looks for answers regarding the disappearance of a 12-year-old pregnant girl; in the French film *Stranger by the Lake*, a lakeside murder is a metaphor for sexual recklessness.

Why do lakes so frequently lend themselves to ominous scenarios and tales of secrecy, caution and loss? Usually, lakes are isolated. They are also stagnant and may have underwater dangers like rocks, tree roots and unpredictable water temperatures. Often the bottom of a lake can't be seen, and its literal mystery and darkness is a great symbol for masked consequence, corruption, repression and peril. History often tells us that lakes harbour spirits and bad memories. At Lake

Minninup in Western Australia and at Reservoir in Victoria, Indigenous people were massacred.

To counter this collective fear of lakes, I've tried to put aside dark thoughts as I set out for Lake Parramatta. I worked in Westmead for several years and I am embarrassed to admit that I didn't know this place existed until a friend who grew up in the area clued me in. Lake Parramatta is a short 2-kilometre bus ride north from the Parramatta CBD and it sits among a beautiful 73-hectare bush reserve of ghost gums, grey boulders, magenta-flecked rock shelves and golden water reeds.

Lake Parramatta is a human-made lake, the result of the building of Australia's oldest dam, which still sits at one end of the swimming area. The dam, known for its beautiful arch-walled stonemasonry, was decommissioned in 1909. The lake was a popular swimming destination from the 1920s to the 1940s but water pollution from nearby industry put an end to swimming for many years. Old-timers speak of seeing chemicals, scum, oil and dead wildlife floating on the water. A motorway was built immediately south of the lake, further diminishing the reputation of this spot as a place of recreation. Happily, the Lake Parramatta area was resuscitated this century and in 2015 the lake was reopened for swimming. Water quality is checked frequently and, as for Sydney Harbour, swimming is only ill advised on days immediately following heavy rain.

The resuscitation of Lake Parramatta was especially welcomed by the 260 000 people of Parramatta who, incredibly, had no public swimming pool for six summers. In 2017, Parramatta lost its venerable Memorial Swimming Pool. The pool, which had been partly funded by the public (swimmers each bought a tile at five shillings apiece), was built in 1959 and was a major social and recreational hub for generations of people. When its demolition was announced by the NSW government to make way for a $300 million stadium, locals protested noisily and colourfully, hanging beach towels and cossies on the pool's wire fences. The pool was free to all on its last day, and hundreds of locals came for a final swim. After their last laps, swimmers wept and embraced each other, and some even took home bottles of pool water. The new Parramatta Aquatic Centre finally opened in 2023.

I've checked the City of Parramatta website for the average water temperatures of Lake Parramatta in May, and I am alarmed to find out that it's 16 degrees. Arriving at the lake, my ambivalence to swimming is offset by the unusually warm and golden autumn afternoon. The reserve around the lake literally glows. Leaves are curling and yellowed, and reeds encircle the water like a flaxen picket fence. Some wattle sprigs have appeared, two months premature. I follow a beautifully landscaped sandstone path that gently tumbles down to the lake and see a swimming enclosure marked by buoys. The setting is entirely bucolic and the antithesis of all my sinister lake associations.

To enter the lake, I need to slide on my bottom down a rock that slopes into the water. The rock's contours are carpeted in furry moss, and suddenly its surface falls away into deep, dark water. I feel like I've climbed into the mouth of a serpent and willingly surrendered myself to its vast belly. There are some half-hidden branches and leaf litter where the water meets the rock, but these soon disappear, and after a stroke or two I can't touch the bottom.

I'm wearing goggles and as I dive under the tea-coloured water, I can't see much. I feel like I'm swimming through a sepia fog, but rather than unnerving me, the monochrome water makes me curious. I want to know if it will remain static or yield visual surprises. I enjoy using the strength of my body to penetrate further into the lake, but several kicks and strokes do nothing to change the colour of the water; it just becomes colder the further I swim. Shrouded in amber water, I think of Margaret Atwood's book *Surfacing*, which is set near a wooded lake in 1960s Quebec. A story of a woman's struggle for identity, the novel is suffused with descriptions of inundation, drowning and surfacing that evoke the unnamed protagonist's losses and convey her emotional states. Fully submerged, I feel as if the lake has become a bush-scented womb, and I am a foetus safely cushioned and nourished by its amniotic fluids. The lake's constant colour holds too many mysteries for me to glean and I am happy just to be among them. Looking up, I see the golden afternoon sun gently stroking the top of the lake's density, and I surface. I throw my head back, take a deep gulp of air and allow the lake to support and swaddle me. I look at the blue sky and the limbs of a glorious gum tree whose leaves catch the breeze.

I take my time to climb out of the water and enjoy the warmth of the sandstone as I let the rocks I'm sitting on absorb my wetness. As the breeze ripples the copper-coloured lake, I hum a favourite piece of classical music and I begin to feel goosebumps. I smile. Rather than crawling with a lake-induced horror or fear, my skin tingles with a feeling of wellness. Today's immersion has bestowed a sense of calm and serenity, washing away my negative preconceptions about lakes.

WINTER

27
RED LEAVES AND ROSE
MURRAY ROSE POOL, DOUBLE BAY

Murray Rose, an Olympic champion of the 1950s and 1960s, was one of Australia's most revered swimming legends. He's part of a pedigree of celebrated male swimmers that stretches from Fred Lane to Kyle Chalmers, and includes Andrew 'Boy' Charlton, David Thiele, Michael Wenden, Kieren Perkins, Grant Hackett and Ian Thorpe. Rose was the poster boy of the 1956 Melbourne Olympics, winning gold medals in the 400 and 1500 metres freestyle, and in the men's 4 × 200 metres freestyle relay. He won gold again in the 400 metres at Rome in 1960, and after Kaylee McKeown, Ian Thorpe, Ariarne Titmus, Shane Gould and Dawn Fraser, has been Australia's most successful Olympic swimmer in individual events.

Rose grew up in Double Bay and as young boy regularly swam at the newly built Redleaf Pool. He had his first swimming lesson here at the age of five, and the enclosed harbour pool soon became his playground. By the age of ten, Rose was breaking records, and by 17 he was an Olympic champion. During his swimming career, he broke 15 world records. Urbane and telegenic, he had a highly successful career as a sports commentator, appeared in films, and worked in the USA in sports branding and promotion. Rose moved back to Sydney in the 1990s, and when he died in 2012, the pool that he'd swum in as a boy was renamed Murray Rose Pool in his honour.

Apart from his direct connection to the pool, it seems fitting that Redleaf is now named after Rose: it's attractive, elegant and sophisticated; it effortlessly sits among the rich and powerful; and it welcomes all.

Murray Rose Pool occupies one of the city's most desired pieces of waterfront real estate. It looks north, spectacularly, across the whole breadth of the harbour, and if you swam in a straight line for about 2 kilometres (as Rose no doubt could), you'd end up at Bradleys Head. The pool sits immediately next door to Fairwater, the mansion on Seven Shillings Beach that was once owned by Lady Mary Fairfax and is now occupied by tech entrepreneur Mike Cannon-Brookes.

One of Sydney's loveliest tidal pools, Murray Rose Pool is a semicircular enclosure of harbour. A shark net, and a narrow, elevated boardwalk around the perimeter keep out unwanted visitors but don't intrude too much on the view to Clark Island, bobbing yachts and the exclusive urban density of Darling Point. Two square wooden pontoons are moored in the middle of the pool. As well as providing places to sunbathe or rest between laps, these are perfect vantage points to see and be seen. There's a small, flat golden beach where toddlers can play, a sloping grassy knoll where residents who have attended one of the area's many laser clinics can display their buffed bodies, and a cafe if swimming isn't your thing.

Murray Rose Pool is a relatively well-kept secret, and locals probably like it that way. It's accessed by steps that lead down from behind the Woollahra Council buildings that are set back some way from New South Head Road. The only indication that something special lies beyond the tall Norfolk Island pines in the council's gardens are two street-side stone columns discreetly bearing the word 'Redleaf' in gold.

Unlike many of Sydney's other harbour beaches, Murray Rose Pool is surrounded by a built environment, rather than by bush reserves. Complementing Lady Fairfax's former digs on the right is an elegant Art Deco apartment building on the left. The apartment block's bricks are red, the colour of an autumn leaf, and its ocean liner–curved bay windows and balconies mirror the contours of the pool's enclosure and evoke the glamour of a Fred Astaire and Ginger Rogers movie. Further along the waterfront are more Deco apartments with private beaches, and opulent mansions. There's a cosmopolitan air to Murray Rose Pool. Its timber pontoons, calm water and proximity to chic apartment buildings remind me of the urban beaches of France's Côte d'Azur such as Beaulieu-sur-Mer.

I'm swimming at Murray Rose on an early June afternoon and, delightfully, red leaves literally float upon the surface of the water. The eastern suburbs' plane trees continue to shed their leaves; borne by soft winds and the city's stormwater system, these russet pieces of natural debris have found a suitable home. The swim is by turns exhilarating and relaxing. While there's a mild chill to the air, the water temperature is still 19 degrees and it's wonderful to be breaststroking through the briny green of the harbour and looking at a panorama of boats, buildings and foliage. I swim some laps of backstroke too, enjoying the cirrus clouds and soft pale blues of a just-turned-winter sky.

In its obituary of Rose, *The New York Times* referred to his freestyle stroke's 'special signature', a 'split-second pause that occurs as he leans on his extended right arm and breathes on his left side, a pause during which he is absolutely relaxed'. I try to approximate this technique in the final couple of laps I swim. Completely ignorant of whether my mimicry is accurate or not, I nonetheless feel a wave of relaxation and calm.

Those who knew Rose have mentioned that his good looks and charisma sometimes distracted people from his decency and conviction. Like his parents, he was a lifelong vegetarian and his diet led to the nickname 'The Seaweed Streak'. In later life, he was a patron for Rainbow Club, a charity that teaches children with a disability to swim, and his championing of masters swimming won the affection of many older Australians.

On his Ocean Pools NSW blog, Simon Duffin recounts an incident at Redleaf in 1951 in which outraged bathers watched a man pull the sleeves of a woollen jumper over his legs and wade into the water. The man was poor and had been washing his clothes in the pool's change rooms. He'd used some coins he'd collected from the deposits of drink bottles to pay for his entrance fee and, not having enough money to buy swimmers, resorted to using the pullover as his togs. Like Charlie Chaplin's Little Tramp character gatecrashing a social grandee's gala, the man caused a spectacle and sent ripples through the sensibilities of the local community. Police were called and the man was eventually removed. The anecdote seems particularly poignant today, when a man in a sleeping bag sleeps rough on the beach. Thankfully, no one is calling the police.

I think about the contrast between the jumper-clad Redleaf bather and Murray Rose, who as a boy might even have been in the crowd that day. I like to think that Rose, a champion of the pool and of people less fortunate than himself, would have treated this man kindly and, like the pool named after him, would have welcomed all.

28
THE GOLDEN GIRLS
ANNETTE KELLERMAN
AQUATIC CENTRE, MARRICKVILLE

Nowadays, it's unlikely that the name 'Esther Williams' would resonate with anyone other than people over 60, cinephiles or fans of artistic swimming. A former American swimming champion, she was discovered by an MGM talent scout and made her name appearing in Hollywood movies in the 1940s and 1950s. Called 'America's Mermaid', she was, in essence, an aquatic showgirl. Donning waterproof make-up and a one-piece, she seemingly held her breath forever as she performed highly choreographed underwater routines. Her films, referred to as 'aqua musicals', contributed to a renaissance in the discipline of artistic swimming and, appropriately, artistic swimming was introduced as an Olympic sport when Los Angeles hosted the Games in 1984. One of Williams' most successful films was the 1952 biopic *Million Dollar Mermaid*. The subject of the hit movie was Sydney's Annette Kellerman.

Born in Marrickville, a 20-minute walk from the pool that was named after her, Annette Kellerman grew up in a late-19th-century bohemian family. She suffered from polio as a child and was prescribed swimming to build her strength. A natural in the water, she was mentored by Olympic gold medallist Fred Lane and quickly became a swimming champion, setting a new women's world record for swimming the mile. After moving to London as a teenager, Kellerman pioneered a performance genre that incorporated underwater ballet, diving and swimming. She was a master of self-promotion and through feats such as a 27-kilometre swim down the Thames, and races across the Seine and Danube Rivers, she became one of Europe's best-known female performers. Dubbed the 'Australian mermaid', she made several highly successful underwater films in the silent era, including *A Daughter of the Gods*, the first film to have a million-dollar budget. Kellerman was a lifelong vegetarian and she followed her film career with a highly successful career in health food retailing. She returned to Australia in 1970, lived on the Gold Coast and died at the age of 89. Her ashes were scattered on the Great Barrier Reef.

It's appropriate that the pool that bears the name of a late-19th-century swimming champ turned silent-movie queen is set among the formal historic beauty of Federation-era Enmore Park. Victorian gas lamps and monumental rows of Canary Island palms adorn the indoor pool's entrance. The pool's glass walls reveal the park, the western sun, and the white-and-brown hues of early-20th-century houses. It's apt that at this aquatic centre named after an underwater star, the main lap pool is at its most beautiful when seen from below the surface of the water. The pool's floor, immaculately clean and tiled in two shades of blue, positively gleams as shafts of afternoon sunshine hit its finish.

I like to think that the spiritual successors to Annette Kellerman and Esther Williams are the groups of ladies who meet today to high-kick, tread water and bob joyously as they go through the motions of their deep water aerobics classes. Led by an instructor who strikes me as a cross between a high school PE teacher and a demanding Broadway choreographer, the class of 15 ladies and two gentlemen strut their stuff with gusto as they flex, kick, paddle and pull to the tunes of Glen Miller, Brahms' 'Lullaby' and Bizet's 'March of the Toreadors'. Discreetly doing my laps a couple of lanes away from these aquatic Rockettes, I enjoy their underwater spectacle. Held afloat with buoyancy belts, the ladies and gents point their toes with the precision of ballerinas and kick their feet in a graceful unison that would make Busby Berkeley, the 1930s American choreographer and film director, proud. The overall mood is akin to an underwater audition as the poolside instructor booms, 'Two-one to the shallow!', 'Two-one to the deep!', 'Up! Out! In! Around!' and 'Five, six, seven, eight!'.

One lady, wearing a bathing cap that is jauntily decorated with three rubber daisies, catches my eye. Accessorising her wonderful cap with an ear-to-ear grin, she, like her floating sisters, is living proof of Kellerman's claim that aquatic fitness is the greatest contributor to lifelong beauty.

29
WILD SWIMMING

GLENBROOK GORGE, BLUE MOUNTAINS NATIONAL PARK

The therapeutic benefits of trees, nature, water and mindfulness have long been documented. When life's daily pressures become cumulative and grinding, a nature-based prescription of purposeful activity in green space is a powerful antidote to stress and anxiety. Dispensing that prescription with the element of water induces even greater healing, and as I watched a very stressed friend visibly reset, I realised that swimming in bushland can be a remarkable remedy for urban angst and uncertainty.

On this Saturday morning in July, a friend of mine, T, is feeling particularly frayed after hours of exasperating and time-consuming house hunting. As T seeks his first Sydney home, he has spent large amounts of his weekends over the last few months successively inspecting small flats and becoming increasingly despondent. Each weekend, he has probed dark or damp or noisy domestic spaces, inhaled the smell of hastily removed pets, listened to empty promises from real estate agents, and fronted up to auctions where he has been outbid by buyers who are more cashed up, more financially aggressive or more self-assured.

Today, I try to offer T some moral support as I follow him in and out of properties that fall within his price range. We view a flat that is berated by busy traffic, a deceased estate decorated with chintz and religious art, and a home that bears the tidy domestic footprints of a lady who has newly been relocated to a nursing home. At one property, a renter – presumably disgruntled by the prospect of his home being sold without any concession to his life or future – launches guerrilla warfare on the prospects of its sale. Cigarette ashes are emphatically strewn across a bathtub, an unflushed toilet dares buyers to linger, and freshly washed undies dangle on hangers in an absolute inversion of the usual pre-sale 'makeover'. The kitchen floor is sticky with grease from months of cooking and the tenant belligerently parks himself on the sofa, shooting each new viewer a scowl. Our admiration for the tenant's passive aggression is quickly erased by an auction at the next property. Here, we look at each other in disbelief as bidders frantically yell six-figure numbers to secure a small and marginally more desirable parcel of strata living.

Having done this drill week after week, T is becoming shell-shocked, and close to the point of retreat. He says Saturdays feel like trench warfare. On Saturday mornings, as online alerts command his attention like an officer blowing a whistle to tell the troops it's time to go over the top, T fixes his bayonet, charges into the fray with a battalion of others, and tries to not get massacred. By 1 pm today, T has had it, and we take refuge at a courtyard cafe to lick wounds and consider the next move. Most of the inspections have finished and we know the law of diminishing returns means that our attention and morale is fading. Sensing that a radical move is needed to assuage the day's barrages, we decide that it's literally time to take to the mountains.

After less than an hour on the M4 motorway, we're at the charming village of Glenbrook in the Lower Blue Mountains. Ten minutes later, we're walking into Glenbrook Gorge in the Blue Mountains National Park. Even though it's mid-afternoon on a winter's day, the gorge is flooded in sunlight and the temperature is mild. We have the gorge entirely to ourselves and we can't decide what is more astonishing – this wonderful detail, the elemental beauty of the place, or the fact that we are just 15 minutes from Penrith.

Glenbrook Gorge has been formed over thousands of years by the movement of Glenbrook Creek, which eventually flows into the Nepean River. The bottom of the narrow valley is pockmarked with craters, some big enough to house a group of picnickers, and the gorge's contours are marked by soaring vertical cliffs. In their marvellous and meticulously researched guidebook *Wild Swimming*, Sally Tertini and Steve Pollard describe this spot as never-ending 'craggy forms of orange and charcoal … that rise up towards the sky, hemming you in'.

Most of the walk involves skipping over rocks and boulders as we follow the flow of the creek. Along the way, little swimming holes successively become larger and more pristine. We hadn't intended to swim today but the sound of the running water and the clarity of the pools seduce, and by the time we reach the fourth swimming hole, we decide we *have* to swim. Giant slabs of rock delineate the largest swimming hole's circumference and they look like the tumbled tombstones of enormous beings. Maybe they are rune stones that were frantically thrown into the sky by a gigantic soothsayer seeking cosmic answers. This place is stupendous and conjures memories of the sacred water pools of Kakadu National Park. The valley exerts a primordial power, and its honeycomb walls feel more shaped by time than by wind or water or other forces of nature. The gorge vibrates and hums.

Stripping off and slightly manic, we scamper over the dark

and slippery slabs of rock towards the pool. In our enthusiasm, we both slip and graze our legs. T suggests that these minor injuries, an offering of our DNA, have been exacted as payment for the right to become part of this breathtaking environment. It seems a fair price to pay for connecting with such a remarkable and restorative setting.

I gasp as I initiate contact with the cold water, immediately feeling its grip on my freshly grazed leg. Yet rather than recoil, I feel beckoned, and I advance into the numbing element. The pool, like the gorge's base, is full of craters so the water's depth varies from waist deep to an indeterminate level. As we swim over sinkholes of inky water, we shudder with more intense waves of cold. The sound of a train making its way from the Blue Mountains down to Sydney shocks me. It seems impossible that such a prosaically urban noise can intrude upon a space that feels so isolated and ancient. Despite its cold tingle, the water's embrace feels immensely healing and it's only the onset of shivers that tells me I should climb out.

The afternoon sun is still warm, and we lie on rocks to dry like the water dragons and skinks that share the swimming hole with us. I feel as if I've just had a deep-tissue massage and I flop to my right-hand side, limbs splayed like bagpipes. T lies on his back and, with every posterior surface of his body touching the rock, he looks as if he has become a contour of its surface. He exhales deeply, drawing energy as well as warmth from the rock. After the exhausting day of house hunting, T seems refreshed and renewed by our wild swimming.

Sydney real estate agents often market the city's enviable lifestyle. Yet today's hamster wheel of inspections, disappointments and stresses seems entirely at odds with a life well lived. The beauty, tranquillity and majesty of Glenbrook Gorge bestow fresh perspective on the day. The valley's sweet, flavoured air, enormous cliffs and invigorating water insist that we take pause and try to see things differently. Our dip in wild water has washed away the day's anxiety and we walk out of the valley feeling hopeful and restored.

30

THE CRYPT

COOK + PHILLIP PARK POOL, SYDNEY

The City of Sydney is justly proud of its sextet of wonderful public pools. But as in most families, not all these aquatic siblings are equally blessed. The harbourside Andrew 'Boy' Charlton Pool has the looks; the eco-friendly, award-winning Prince Alfred Park Pool has the brains; the sleek, Harry Seidler–designed Ian Thorpe Aquatic Centre has the style; Victoria Park Pool, an oasis in a 9-hectare park, has the soul; and the newest addition, Gunyama Park Aquatic and Recreation Centre in Zetland, like most late-arrival youngest children, has been spared no expense and is spoiled rotten. That leaves the Cook + Phillip Park Pool. It has water-stained concrete.

To be fair, the Cook + Phillip pool is clean, well maintained and staffed efficiently by friendly young people. In addition to a 50-metre main pool, it has a kids' pool presided over by a giant, fun, mosaic sea serpent, a courtyard garden with sun lounges, a cafe and a hydrotherapy pool. It would be a perfectly acceptable indoor pool in many other cities. But when compared to its pin-up pool siblings, it's the runt of the Sydney litter.

Commissioned prior to the 2000 Sydney Olympic Games, the Cook + Phillip was beset by controversy even before it was constructed. Built on the site where a bowling green once stood, it sits, like a crypt, literally under the piazza that fronts St Mary's Cathedral. Would any city other than Sydney dare to erect an aquatic centre under the parvis of its main Catholic cathedral? Even our sister cities in hedonism, San Francisco, Barcelona and Rio de Janeiro, would baulk at this sybaritic audacity. But maybe in an age of growing secularism, its erection here is entirely apt. Who is the more worshipped in 21st-century Sydney? The body, the cafe, the lifestyle – or Mary MacKillop's statue and the bishops of Rome?

The design intention of the piazza that is supported by the roof of the aquatic centre was to create a new public space for the city. On most days, its granite, treeless, sometimes graffitied expanse is populated by seagulls, pigeons, ibises and the occasional skateboarder. The pool and fitness centre below is accessed, like all crypts, via a set of many stairs. Architect and writer Laura Harding has described the pool as 'buried in deference to parkland and civic monuments'. The pool has a subterranean mood, but not one that is cosy or womblike. The main roof, giant western wall and buttresses are all dark cement, and large blotches of discolouring are the result of leaks and water stains. A similar mood pervades the change rooms. A gay friend wag has nicknamed Cook + Phillip 'Cock and Feel It' because of the communal shower space in the men's change rooms, which apparently generates some after-swim activity. I wonder if this recounted history at the pool also mirrors activities that have allegedly taken place in the precincts of St Mary's.

Not all of Cook + Phillip is a concrete bunker. The eastern wall of the pool's complex is glass, which lets in lots of morning sun, as well as affording views of the foliage of Cook + Phillip Park. However, on the dark winter's afternoon when I visit, very little natural light enters the main pool area, and the mood is sombre and muted. At the very top of the high western wall, a small skirting of skylights reveals a few momentary and frustrating glimpses of the city above: a disembodied frond from a palm tree, the transitory legs of a moving pedestrian. The acute divorce of the swimmers from these hints of city life makes me think of Daniel Libeskind's remarkable architecture in the Jewish Museum in Berlin. One of the most confronting aspects of Libeskind's building is an axis that leads to a 24-metre bare and empty concrete tower that is neither heated nor cooled. Its only access to the light and sounds of the city streets above come from a tiny slit in its roof, and its overwhelming mood is one of claustrophobia, alienation and anxiety.

Crypts are silent, austere places, yet they inevitably contain artistic treasures, be they reliquaries containing the bones of saints, pious paintings or the sculptural tombs of rulers. In the crypt of St Mary's a few hundred metres from the Cook + Phillip pool, the solemn cavernous area is decorated with a terrazzo floor featuring a motif of the Celtic cross. It is considered one of the finest 20th-century mosaic floors in the world, and it greatly lifts an otherwise funereal space.

It is likely that early in the pool's planning stages, Sydney's burghers became aware of the alienating possibilities of a dark underground pool. To remedy this, they commissioned some oversized and stunning artworks to brighten things up in the crypt-like pool. Sydney artist Wendy Sharpe was chosen to paint eight gigantic portraits depicting the life of Marrickville-born swimming champion and silent film star Annette Kellerman. The panels, each one 4.8 metres in length, are picture-book playful and vibrantly colourful. They show Kellerman as an Edwardian world record-holder, a vaudeville performer, a silent film star and a contented Gold Coast retiree. Whether diving into the Seine to outrace men or being arrested for daring to bare her legs on a Boston beach, Kellerman was larger than life, and Wendy Sharpe's deliberately overstated portraits wonderfully convey this. For more than two decades they enlivened the pool, until one winter morning, staff discovered a panel dangling perilously, like the sword of Damocles, above the pool, and all eight had to be removed.

Crypts are places that evoke contemplation in visitors, as thoughts turn to mortality and to the righteous acts of noble humans who have been laid in earth. At Cook + Phillip, it is the swimmers who are interred in water and invited to contemplate. Encased in the cool blue water of the lap pool, we move silently up and down, drawn intensely into an aquatic meditation that is made more extreme by the sensory deprivations of the building.

As I swim, my mind turns to many things: to thoughts of my health, my family, my friends; to musings on faith, justice, politics and love. And then, these thoughts are pleasantly splintered by the recollection of Annette Kellerman who famously yelled 'Cooee!' before she brazenly dived into the pool of the London Hippodrome. This detail makes me smile and I am reminded that beyond the darkness and restraint of all crypts lie the colour and vigour and joy of the living.

31
NOBODY'S GONE SURFING
NORTH NARRABEEN ROCK POOL

Those of us who aren't Beach Boys aficionados or from the Northern Beaches might be surprised to hear that Narrabeen Beach was immortalised in a Beach Boys song. In the 1963 megahit 'Surfin' U.S.A.', the phrase 'Australia's Narabine' is used in the song's second verse as a rhyme to 'Ventura County Line'. Narrabeen is the only non-American beach mentioned in the song. While the song's reference to Narrabeen is misspelled and awkwardly rhymed, it is an acknowledgement of the Sydney surfing culture that was already strongly established in the post–World War II years, and attests to the fact that young men here also wore 'baggies' and had 'bushy bushy blond hairdos'.

The Hawaiians gave the world the gift of surfing and a Hawaiian was one of the first people to draw widespread attention to surfing in Sydney. Olympic swimming champion Duke Kahanamoku (whose statue stands at Freshwater Beach) wowed beachgoers with a surfing display in 1914. The title of 'Australia's first surfer' was often given to Isabel Letham, a 14-year-old girl who was randomly picked from a crowd to ride tandem with Kahanamoku in one of his demonstrations. Letham went on to teach swimming in the US, and her fascinating life is recounted in Yves Rees' marvellous book, *Travelling to Tomorrow*. However, before Letham ever set foot on a surfboard, a tight-knit group of surfers that included female riders Isma Amor and Doris Stubbins had been surfing at Manly. The oldest known image of anyone in Australia surfing is of a merchant sailor called Tommy Walker who, in the summer of 1911–12, was famous for doing headstands on his large wooden board.

Regardless of who actually introduced surfing to Sydney, it quickly caught on and by the 1950s there was a strong local surfers' subculture. Young surfers in Sydney both consumed the music and cinema of international surfer culture and contributed to it. In the same year that 'Surfin' U.S.A.' hit the charts, a Sydney band called The Atlantics had a local number one hit with their surfie instrumental 'Bombora'. Large dances in surf lifesaving clubs known as 'stomps' brought thousands of young surfers together to dance to tunes like Little Pattie's 'He's My Blonde-Headed, Stompie Wompie, Real Gone Surfer Boy'. Sydney surfer tribalism grew in the 1970s and its counterculture was expressed in surfer movies, psychedelically painted panel vans, a pervasive drug scene and obsessive loyalty to local bands like 'The Oils' and 'Aussie Crawl'. The novel *Puberty Blues* and its film version capture this cocktail of surfing, machismo and hedonism.

In his memoir *The Boy Behind the Curtain*, Tim Winton talks about surfing as 'an expression of youthful vigour, engagement with nature, lust for life'. He also writes of the special kinship and lingo of surfers, who crave 'flow', a life alternative to the 'symmetry, linear order, solid boundaries' of conventional life. Surfing, Winton argues, involves the letting go of timetables and a submission to nature. I've never been a surfer but the surfers I know similarly speak of their lifelong addiction to the waves, their camaraderie, and of how surfing takes them into a 'zone' that is removed from time and the constraints of daily life.

Today I've come to North Narrabeen to feel some 'flow' from a distance. The surf break of North Narrabeen is one of the most iconic surfing spots in Sydney and it is widely considered to be the best surfing beach on the Northern Beaches. Some surfers say that when it is at its best, it's the premier break in Australia. This is partly to do with the geography of the beach. A sandbank sits at the mouth of the Narrabeen Lakes, and it helps to create consistently huge and rideable waves. North Narrabeen is one of 19 national surfing reserves and, along with Maroubra, Cronulla and Manly-Freshwater, is one of the few found in Sydney.

Local wisdom holds that North 'Narra' is only for the experienced. Australia's first two world surfing champions, Midget Farrelly and Nat Young, both honed their skills at its break. North Narrabeen's barrels have continued to draw legends like Mark Warren, Damien Hardman, Ozzie Wright, Layne Beachley and Sally Fitzgibbons. The beach's Boardriders Club, established in 1964, is the oldest in Sydney and the second oldest in Australia (after Phillip Island in Victoria), and its alumni list includes many national and international surfing champions.

Excited by the beach's pedigree and with much expectation about the quality of local surfing I'd see at Narrabeen, I am astonished to find no surfers at the beach. I'd taken a B1 double-decker bus from Wynyard and amusedly watched a young man insouciantly carry his waxed surfboard up to the top deck and plonk it on the seat next to him as if it were a modest bag of groceries. Jumping off the bus at Narrabeen, I noticed that the surfer and some other backpackers were staying on the bus, perhaps headed for Warriewood or Mona Vale further up the coast. Maybe they knew something that I didn't.

After walking a couple of blocks, past some flats, a few old shacks and large suburban houses that fly Australian flags in their front gardens, I come to the long beach. Its sand is the colour of chewable vitamin C tablets and it dramatically slopes down to powerful, churning surf. On this sunny and mild July Monday, I have the entire long stretch of the beach to myself, save for a tradie picnicking on his lunch break and a young couple walking the beach with their baby in a backpack. At 3.6 kilometres, Narrabeen-Collaroy is Sydney's second-longest beach (after Cronulla), and even though it is a weekday I had assumed that this long rolling break and the relatively mild weather would draw some surfers.

It turns out that today's waves are mostly closeouts, so surfers are staying away. Closeouts are waves that break all at once from end to end. Instead of peeling to provide a surfer entry to a rideable, tubular wave from left to right (or vice versa), closeouts crest and fall parallel to the shore and only allow the surfer to ride straight into the beach. As well as being dud waves to ride, closeouts can be physically dangerous and can smash a board to bits.

I'm often impressed (and envious) of surfers' knowledge of the waves, the sea and weather conditions in general. Surfers tell me that a key skill in their sport is knowing how to read the break. Meteorology and physics go some way in helping to understand waves: wind and tide forecasts and swell periods will predict how big a break might be and how much energy is in a wave, and this information is obviously useful for analysing how waves will build and travel. But most surfers don't use physics to suss out if the waves are worth surfing. Wind direction, swell size and water colour are the most used rules of thumb for assessing a break. If these elements aren't in harmony (as they're not today), it's best to stay away.

The potential power of Narrabeen's waves is legendary. In 2016, a king tide and storm surges eroded 50 metres of Narrabeen's beach. During the surge, the backyards of waterfront houses in neighbouring Collaroy were swallowed by the tide, swimming pools were uprooted and back rooms were hammered by waves. With extraordinary weather events becoming more regular, I wonder what impacts climate change may have on the beach, and whether more storm surges might wipe out houses and smash the foreshore in the same way that a closeout can wipe out a surfer and snap a board.

With no surfers to admire and dumping waves rolling unrelentingly into the beach, there's only one option for today: a swim in the safely enclosed North Narrabeen Rock Pool. To get there from the beach, I need to walk around the Narrabeen Lagoon, which is home to some charming aquatic birdlife. A pelican the height of a small child sits on a sandbar in the lagoon and seems entirely unperturbed as I wade out towards it to get a better look. As I admire it, and the herons and cormorants and plovers, I marvel at how easily this city offers up a mini coastal holiday in return for a 45-minute bus ride and a few dollars off my Opal card.

Jutting out into the rolling waves, the North Narrabeen Rock Pool is a pool within a pool. The larger 70-by-40-metre pool is surrounded by roaring surf on its east and south sides, and by the lagoon on its west. It's more of a wading pool than a space for laps and its bottom surface is irregular, reflecting the contours of the rock shelf onto which it was grafted. The larger pool encloses a smaller 50-by-18-metre lap pool that has eight lanes. A wooden boardwalk that hovers just above the water's surface partitions one pool from the other and marks the lap pool's northern and eastern perimeters. An original feature from the 1930s that has been restored many times because of wild seas, the boardwalk allows non-swimmers to literally walk on water and stand Jesus-like in the middle of the whole complex. Like many of Sydney's rock pools, these pools were built as part of the employment relief scheme during the Depression. What foresight to use public works as both a source of employment and the endowment of such an amenity.

One other swimmer shares the lap pool with me today and we smile and nod as we sometimes surface at one of the pool's ends at the same time. We're careful not to cramp each other's style, and even though waves wash over the lips of the pool, we can still swim in a straight line. As we towel off, we compare notes on the ocean temperature and how fortunate we are to have this all to ourselves. I mention that I had come to Narrabeen to catch some of its famed surfers in action, and my fellow swimmer responds, matter-of-factly, 'Nah, nobody's surfin' today, mate, not with those waves.' He pauses for a moment, looks at the surf, looks at the pool, smiles and then adds, 'And why would you surf when you could swim?'

32
BRIDGES

NATIONAL CENTRE OF
INDIGENOUS EXCELLENCE, REDFERN

The National Centre of Indigenous Excellence (NCIE) sits on the land of the Gadigal people of the Eora Nation, in the heart of Redfern. It's a not-for-profit social enterprise where First Nations peoples can access opportunities to improve holistic wellbeing, deepen cultural connection and achieve greater economic empowerment.

The centre's gym and pool is a modern facility that shines with pride and buzzes with activity. An honour roll of Indigenous Olympians and Paralympians greets visitors and reminds them that excellence is an expectation. Group gym and aquatic classes are designed to be culturally appropriate to First Nations groups, who make up a quarter of the membership. The 25-metre pool is sleek, sparkling and heated all year round. Here, new swimmers of any age are given one-on-one or group instruction, and everyone is welcome. Inclusion and fun are important elements of the learn-to-swim classes.

On this winter's day, I am feeling cold and fatigued. I'm relieved to see that that the pool is covered in a translucent canopy that keeps the wind out but lets the light in. It's an appealing space with a small, west-facing terrace that looks out on to the centre's generous playing fields and the back streets of Redfern. A large mural along the soccer pitch reads

'Traditional Smoke Heals, Tobacco Smoke Kills', echoing a key message of the centre's TATU (Talking About Tobacco Use) program that successfully works to reduce smoking rates among Indigenous communities.

Like the pool, much of the design of the NCIE is beautiful, considered and layered with meaning. The centre sits on the former site of Redfern Primary School, and its Victorian, heritage-listed buildings – which now house the venues for conferences and workshops – act as an architectural bridge between past and present learning. In front of the pool and gym complex are grass trees, welcoming the visitor and marking the first iteration of a collection of bush tucker trees from around Australia that have been planted throughout the centre. As well as referencing nourishment, resilience and sustainability, the multi-state provenance of the trees reminds us that this is a national centre of learning.

I've hit the pool at a time when there's a lull in classes so I'm lucky enough to have a lane to myself, and with it the mental space to assuage my sense of fatigue and enjoy some contemplative swimming. It's NAIDOC Week – the week that Indigenous peoples celebrate their histories, cultures and achievements – and as I swim at the NCIE, I reflect on the resilience and generosity of First Nations people in this city. I'm always astonished when Elders offer a Welcome to Country to people who are descendants of those who made their ancestors dispossessed. I am similarly moved by decades of First Nations resistance to the occupation of their land and by their ongoing celebration of culture.

NAIDOC Week is a huge deal at the NCIE. It includes a smoking ceremony and the sounds of Koori Radio over loudspeakers as crowds fill conference rooms, and food trucks and stalls animate the courtyard. NAIDOC Week has its historical roots in the Day of Mourning of 1938. With events on a different theme each year, it builds constructively on the heartfelt protest of 1938 and celebrates Indigenous accomplishment, resilience and excellence.

The first few years of this decade at the NCIE were challenging – Covid closures, financial uncertainty, the disappointment at the result of the Voice referendum – but today there's a palpable feeling of determination and pride. I talk with Nate Merritt, First Nations man, and fitness and aquatics duty manager, about how the NCIE pool and gym create and develop an ongoing sense of excellence. 'It's about giving an opportunity to everyone,' Nate says, 'and then watching that excellence and leadership ripple throughout to the broader community.' Nate is justly proud of specific programs such as Active Elders, Mums and Bubs, and the Young, Fit & Deadly wellbeing program for 9–16-year-olds. Offering First Nations people access to fitness and wellness education, the centre builds their confidence and capability, 'with culture at the core'.

The NCIE is a profound bridge between First Nations young people and their full potential, and between Indigenous and non-Indigenous Australians. The pool and gym are open to everyone and almost 200000 people use the centre's facilities each year. A swim here, and a light meal afterwards, directly fund programs that build long-term improvements in the lives of Sydney's First Nations people.

As my body and mind relaxes in this beautiful facility, I recall the vision of the NCIE to create an excellent Australia for all. The pool is a bridge to our best selves, and the centre – a hub for pride, equality, growth and culture – is a bridge to historical reckonings and better futures.

33
WADE

MARRINAWI COVE, BARANGAROO

In the winter before Covid turned the world upside down, I bought myself a wetsuit. Sleekly encased in neoprene and feeling like a newly weaned seal pup, I spent that winter discovering the immense joys of cold-water swimming. A few months later – just before the pandemic made us all work and learn and live and socialise in radically unfamiliar ways – I met my partner.

During the two years of the pandemic's restrictions, closed borders and vaccination rollouts, my beloved and I were gifted time to get to know each other. Unconstrained by other competing social obligations, we looked and lived more inwardly and became each other's world. Like others around the planet, we spent much of this strange time talking, reading, watching TV, cooking, and checking in on friends and family. We were lucky enough to be marooned in a house with a large garden that was a ten-minute walk to a beach. If you didn't linger afterwards, it was permissible to swim at this beach during the lockdowns and, ritualistically donning my wetsuit, I'd swim daily throughout the winter months.

Apart from the beneficial exercise of the swims, I found our winter visits to the sea hugely therapeutic. Exploring underwater habitats reassured me that not all biotic activity was governed by restriction or in a state of anxiety. Sea animals moved as they pleased and with abandon. One afternoon, after a winter swim, I was heartened but unsurprised to read that just five minutes by the sea can strengthen our self-esteem, mood and general mental health.

The winter swims of the pandemic seem like decades ago. Life has seemingly returned to its pre-Covid rhythms, and we're revenge-travelling and live-performance-bingeing like there's no tomorrow. On 8 August 2022 (a day considered incomparably lucky by Chinese people), Crown Casino at Barangaroo opened its doors to VIP punters, and the high rollers' fortunes, on which the building had placed its bets, flowed into the coffers.

One legacy of the pandemic that didn't involve consumption was the realisation that our cities needed more civic space, both green and blue. To that end, Marrinawi Cove, in the north-west corner of Barangaroo Reserve, was opened to public swimming. It's the first swimming spot west of the Harbour Bridge to open in more than 50 years, and moves are afoot within harbourside councils to open similar swimming venues.

Until Rob Stokes, the former NSW Minister for Cities, and local state MP Alex Greenwich dived fully clothed into the harbour at the cove's launch in January 2023, it had been forbidden to swim in this former industrial site. When most of the maritime-industry facilities decamped from the harbour and Barangaroo became prime real estate, overall water quality improved enormously. The 700-square-metre enclosure has a shark net, a shower and, appropriately, toilets in a former nearby sewage pumping station. In a city infamous for hi-vis vests and overregulation, it's astonishing that Marrinawi Reserve is unpatrolled. Even dogs can swim here!

Today my partner and I approach Marrinawi Cove from Wynyard Station. Hopping on a busy city train, navigating corridors of slick LED advertising and traversing a canyon of huge office towers is a strange prelude to a harbour swim. With its sleek corporate lobbies, brand-name shops and franchise eateries, this corner of the Sydney harbourfront feels more like Dubai or Singapore than Woolloomooloo or Balmain. Twisting like a malevolent glass tornado, the Crown Sydney building completely dominates the precinct and makes the substantial ficus trees below its black hulk look tiny. Much has been said and written of how public land ended up as a towering casino and apartment building for VIPs, and of the roles played by a former prime minister, a former NSW premier, a radio shock jock and a billionaire gambling tycoon. To express my feelings for the development, I literally turn my back on the building as we walk to Barangaroo Reserve.

The precinct is freighted with much more historical ballast than the casino controversy. Its namesake, Barangaroo, was a Cammeraygal woman who, like many senior women in her matriarchal society, was a hunter and a provider. Her first husband was said to have died of smallpox, a plague brought by the colonisers that ravaged Sydney's First Nations people, and her second husband was Bennelong. She witnessed the brutal impacts of early colonisation and surprised the British when she defiantly threatened to flog a colonial executioner when she saw him flogging a convict. Unlike Bennelong, Barangaroo refused to dine with the governor of the NSW colony.

With occupation, the lands of this part of the harbour subsequently housed the wharves from which the colony's first exports were loaded, along with a gasworks, berths for the clippers that facilitated the wool trade, the Hungry Mile of the Depression, and a 1960s container terminal.

At the cove, I consciously decide to focus on its beauty. Honey-coloured slabs of sandstone, hewn from the nearby Cutaway, are arranged unevenly around the swimming enclosure like an ancient amphitheatre. The lower slabs are stained emerald-green and burgundy by the seagrass and water. It's a cool July weekday morning, so my partner and I have the place to ourselves, and it feels surreal to be watched by giant glass office towers, and survey the Harbour Bridge and Luna Park as I change into my wetsuit. My partner has decided he's sitting this swim out, and as I put on my goggles, he dives into today's Wordle.

Entering the water from the irregular and sometimes slippery slabs requires dexterity, core strength and patience. The overcast day and the harbour's dark-green opaqueness hide most detail below the water, even where it is most shallow. Initially, this is frustrating. The water is cold on my bare feet, and I become impatient as I register that several of the slabs are encrusted with sharp oyster shells. I realise that to push myself beyond caution, I need to slow down and make a more meaningful connection to the sea. To access water deep enough to swim in, I first need to wade.

Wading is, by its definition, an act of patience and attention. It's a quiet, gentle but persistent advance, a calm prelude to a swim, an act of some difficulty but one of ultimate progress.

Now up to my waist and ready to take my first strokes in the harbour, I turn around and see my partner smiling with encouragement. He's a man of composure, tranquillity and gentleness, and someone who knows how to distil the world into its elemental essentials. As we talked during the long days and nights of the Covid lockdowns, he told me that two things he couldn't live without are fruit and sunshine. His name is Wade.

34
GRAND DESIGN
PRINCE ALFRED PARK POOL, SURRY HILLS

One winter afternoon, as I worked from home and rain fell torrentially, I felt an overwhelming sense of cabin fever. Like a marathon swimmer pushing themself through the pain barrier, I summoned all my reserves of discipline to keep working. Wondering when the deluge might end, I recalled these words from Catherine M Brennan's sublime poem 'Beneath the Deluge':

> Imagine forty days and nights of it:
> attic beams as ships timbers,
> these walls sturdy in heavy seas.
> Adrift, we'd have no choice, would
> rise and sink upon these waves,
> follow the pull of new tides.

I live in a built-up part of Surry Hills, and the incessant sheets of rain and dark clouds that had cocooned the city made my neighbourhood, my home, and the room I was working in feel oppressive and claustrophobic. The damp walls of my home felt like clammy skin, and I was hungry for open space and exercise. I felt that if I couldn't get out of the house soon, I might go quietly mad. As this urge built to its crescendo, the rain suddenly stopped and without a moment's deliberation I grabbed a towel, goggles and swimmers and walked five minutes to my heated outdoor neighbourhood pool in Prince Alfred Park.

For my money, Prince Alfred Park Pool is the pool that most successfully celebrates public urban space in Sydney. On a grey and oppressive day such as this one, the pool's clean lines, ridges of native meadow and cleverly triangulated green perimeters are a godsend. Co-designed and realised by a team of architects and landscape architects in what academic and writer Professor Philip Goad calls a 'collaborative piece of landscape urbanism', the pool privileges landscape over all other design considerations. Entering the pool feels a bit like walking through the Siq, the narrow and mysterious entrance to the ancient city of Petra. Once inside, the noises and intrusions of a busy city seem to disappear, replaced by a softened, 'walled' and enchanted haven of recreation, greenery, light, warmth and space.

When it was conceived as the centrepiece of a major upgrade of Prince Alfred Park, the pool's key conviction was that green space would be sacred. Unlike Andrew 'Boy' Charlton Pool or North Sydney Pool, which are blessed with outrageously sublime locations, or Victoria Park Pool, which sits in the folds of a beautifully landscaped and venerable park, Prince Alfred Park pool, prior to its 2012 upgrade, sat in a flat, largely denuded, unloved public space that felt menacing at night. The principal mission of the park and pool's renewal was to give beautifully designed recreational spaces to one of the city's densest urban neighbourhoods.

Prince Alfred Park has had a chequered history. Before the park was even a twinkle in a surveyor's eye, dense bushland and a tributary of Blackwattle Creek covered the site. When Europeans arrived, the area came to be known as Cleveland

Paddocks, after Cleveland House, which was built in the 1820s and attributed to Francis Greenway. The grand colonial house still stands on the corner of Bedford and Buckingham Streets, and today has unobstructed views to the meadow ridge that encloses the swimming pool. Indigenous people, who had previously been displaced from their traditional campgrounds around Sydney Cove, camped on Cleveland Paddocks until they were again pushed further to the fringes of the city with the coming of the railway and the construction of nearby Central Station in the 1850s.

Despite being described as a 'plague spot' and a 'quagmire with a filthy drain', the Paddocks were earmarked for a showground for the Royal Agricultural Society and named in honour of Queen Victoria's second son. While visiting Sydney in 1868, Alfred survived an assassination attempt and, in a fit of colonial embarrassment, a number of public places and buildings were named after the imperilled prince. A grand Victorian folly was built in 1870 for a Centenary Exhibition to mark Captain James Cook's landing in Botany Bay, and the building, which later housed the Australian War Memorial Museum before it moved to Canberra, sat here until 1954. A pool was first constructed in the park the same year that the Centenary Exhibition building was demolished. It was a stark and tired-looking venue, marooned in an island of cement, and for almost 35 years it competed for patronage with a shabby, tented ice rink next door.

The new pool that opened in Prince Alfred Park in 2013, and which has subsequently won a swag of architectural design awards, has done much to resuscitate the park and make amends for the poor urban planning of the past. The pool's brilliant design team was led by architect Rachel Neeson and landscape architect Sue Barnsley. By literally enfolding much of the space in greenery, they have concealed the pool from the park's other users and created a swimming area that optimises warmth in the winter months, shelters swimmers from the wind, and allows for interaction with landscaping that varies during the seasons. Change rooms, a kiosk, an office and a plant room are cleverly built into a sloping mound that rises up like a wave from Chalmers Street, and which is covered in native meadow grasses. On the pool's west side, a forest of bright-yellow geometric umbrellas playfully adds to the pool's sense of privacy, and behind them sits another rising mound of folded greenery into which (on the park side) is embedded a slippery dip for kids. A copse of Chinese elms contains the pool's southern end, and the deciduous trees here invite the seasons to express themselves.

Despite its wonderful sense of exclusion from the noise and activity of nearby Central Station, the pool is without doubt an urban pool. Sunning themselves on the Chalmers Street side of the pool or reclining on a sun lounge on the pool's southern lawn, swimmers can look beyond the greenery to the towers of Central Sydney. Appropriately, the most prominent landmark from here is Jean Nouvel and Patrick Blanc's remarkable, soaring One Central Park apartment building, which hosts a gigantic and whimsical vertical garden. The pool's swimmers throughout the week are mostly urbanites: office workers clocking up lunchtime laps, tattooed millennials, Queer people, private school girls doing squad training, residents of the nearby Northcott housing estate, young parents holding phones and flat whites while their toddlers learn to swim. With its clever lines, sensuousness, human diversity and vivid colours, it's the sort of pool that Jeffrey Smart and David Hockney would love to paint.

After a couple of days of constant rain, the pool has the freshness of a lake. The Germans use the term *Süßwasser* (or 'sweet water') to differentiate freshwater lakes and rivers from the sea, and on this grey day the pool literally tastes sweet. Maybe the rain has further softened the otherwise very gently chlorinated pool, or maybe the relief and joy that I feel as I unkink and glide up and down the blue lanes of this landscaped aquatic oasis have simply penetrated all my senses, including my sense of taste. A half-hour in this brilliantly conceived pool has been transformative: my mood has morphed from a state of anxiety to one of delight. What a gift to busy Sydney these grand designers have given.

35
SWIMMING WITH FRANKIE
PACIFIC SWIM SCHOOL, CROWS NEST

Every Monday at lunchtime, Frankie goes swimming. Aside from the cardiovascular benefits associated with Frankie's swimming, her aquatic routine improves coordination and balance, and helps her to build muscle tone. Frankie generally eats and sleeps better on the days she has a swim. She also feels calmer and happier. Frankie is six months old.

Like Frankie, thousands of babies learn to swim every week in Sydney at pools such as the Pacific Swim School in Crows Nest. The pool is lined with rubber duckies of various sizes, a large mural of sea creatures is a backdrop to the pool, and opposite is decking, on which rellies or friends like me can sit on stools to watch, laugh and wave. The complex is equipped with change tables, a play corner and a large TV.

Frankie is the daughter of an old friend and former housemate of mine. She's an only child and greatly loved by an extended circle of 'uncles' and 'aunts'. She enjoys a full and stimulating life of playing peekaboo, being read to, playing with her food and rolling from side to side. It's an exciting time for her and for her carers, and a highlight of her week is when her father's dear friend Uncle Robbie takes her swimming. Frankie is at the delightful age where she has just started to focus her attention on faces, and her expressions of recognition, wonder and sometimes puzzlement are precious. Today, cradled safely in Uncle Robbie's calm and capable arms, she seems undaunted by the noise, lights, smells and humidity of the indoor pool.

Frankie is a 'Seahorse'. The Seahorse lessons for three-to-nine-month-old babies focus on building bubs' confidence in the water by bonding with a parent or carer in the pool, and gently getting them familiar with the sensations of the water through play and songs. The lessons gradually teach babies some breath-control techniques and work towards submerging them and encouraging them to float independently.

At ten months old, 'Seahorses' become 'Squids', and then at age two or three, they may progress to becoming 'Clownfish' or 'Angelfish'. If little ones really take to the water, have a natural ability for stroke development and can be in the water independently, they may evolve into 'Sea Dragons', 'Penguins' or 'Otters'.

Frankie's class today is intimate – just three 'Seahorses', each with a parent or carer, and a vivacious instructor with an infectious sense of fun. The instructor uses a doll to indicate to the adults, who are holding the babies in one metre of water, what they need to do. It's a truly immersive experience for both baby and carer. As in a good Pixar movie, the teacher occasionally throws a funny to the adults by encouraging the doll to do a manic swan dive or dance along the water's surface. As Uncle Robbie takes Frankie through a half-hour routine, I laugh out loud as Frankie's faces registers the different sensations of wetness, splashing and floating.

The session begins with Robbie using a brightly coloured plastic cup to playfully pour water over Frankie as he sings 'It's raining, it's pouring, the old man is snoring'. Frankie is encouraged to mimic Uncle Robbie as he reaches for and grabs coloured balls while singing more songs. Entranced by the floating balls, Frankie focuses all her attention on stretching and splashing in the water to get towards them, and the instructor tells us that this activity builds an awareness of movements that in time will develop into the strokes needed for swimming. The activity that most intrigued me was a game in which Robbie sings 'Humpty Dumpty' while Frankie is lifted up off a floating mat with cartoon-like sound effects and then lowered back into the pool. As she hits the water with a hilarious look of disbelief, Robbie is instructed to immediately turn Frankie around towards the mat. This teaches her to instinctively turn around and reach back towards the edge of a pool, rather than to move more perilously further away. The class winds down with a rendition of 'If you're happy and you know it, splash your hands', and an aquatic version of 'The Hokey Pokey'.

Many parents might baulk at the idea of teaching babies as young as three months to swim. Apart from the hassles of pool nappies, cold change rooms and chlorine in little ones' eyes, it might seem counterintuitive, as well as highly stressful for parents and babies, to teach bubs to swim before they can even crawl. Yet, having spent the first nine months of their development floating in the womb, there is a surprising logic to developing babies' aquatic skills as early as possible. Babies have instinctive buoyancy skills, and an in-born kicking reflex that they tend to lose at 12 months. Aquatic activity engages a baby's body in a completely unique way, and the movements learned in water develop catching and grasping skills as well as strengthening core muscles.

The brain activity required as a baby kicks, splashes and glides is said to significantly aid overall cognitive development. As a baby's brain registers the tactile sensation of water and its resistance, it also lays the neurological foundations for later skills such as spatial awareness, language and academic learning. Studies have suggested that babies and infants who learn to swim are more likely to be ahead of their non-swimming peers in mathematics, counting and reading.

The social experience of learning to swim is also said to greatly benefit babies and infants. By interacting with their parents or carers, each other and a swimming instructor in the water, very young children are exposed to the experience of group learning in a playful context. A German study of children who learned swimming from a young age found that they were more independent and self-confident, had greater self-discipline and were socially more comfortable than their non-swimming peers.

Many parents say that bath time is one of the highlights of caring for young children. No doubt the fun and positive associations of bath time play contribute to this belief. The skin-on-skin contact, cuddling and splashing that occurs at bath time is also an element of babies' first experiences of swimming, and this may account for many of the emotional benefits that are attributed to early-life swim lessons. Uncle Robbie enjoys his time with Frankie because it keeps them in the moment and builds a relationship through touch, play and togetherness.

The most obvious benefit of learning to be comfortable in the water at a very early age is infant water safety. Children who are not exposed to water as bubs are more likely to feel anxious in the water later. They are also more resistant to putting their faces underwater and to floating on their backs. Both these skills are key to water safety strategies. Obviously, all children, especially the very young, require a high degree of supervision while in the water, and babies can drown in a couple of centimetres of water. However, babies who have had experience of the water and have been taught to float are much more likely to survive an accident in which they find themselves in water.

Many of my happiest childhood memories involve situations in which I was wet or dripping: eating Twisties and paddle-pops and lollies at the local pool, riding a dumper on a canvas surf mat (the 1970s version of a boogie board), jumping from tree limbs and rocks into a river, skipping from rock pool to rock pool in search of crabs or sea urchins. I naturally took to the water and have been enjoying it all my life. But many children don't like it, and will never overcome anxiety borne from pools, rivers and the ocean to enjoy aquatic memories. Watching Frankie smile and gurgle in the pool, I wonder if there would be fewer aquaphobic children and adults if there were more Uncle Robbies to cradle babies gently in a pool and sing 'If you're happy and you know it, splash your hands'.

36
SAFE HARBOUR
A HAVEN FOR ASYLUM SEEKERS

In a suburban Sydney pool, whose name for confidentiality reasons cannot be disclosed, a group of asylum seekers meet twice a week to relax and enjoy the water. The swimming group consists largely of women and children who have left their countries, their families, their occupations and their identities because of war, persecution, violence and death threats. They come from various countries, and share the daily anxieties of uncertain residency status, precarious housing, lack of work and financial insecurity. Swimming is part of a recreation program that seeks to allay some of this anxiety: it is hoped that when they are in the water, the group can live in the moment and, if only for an hour, forget some of their worries.

In keeping with the pastoral policies of the organisation that coordinates the swimming program, no poolside questions are asked about clients' past lives or their home countries. Discussions of visas and work, and the details of their life challenges, are left at the pool's turnstiles. A premium is placed on wellbeing, relaxation and fun. Conversation is optional, and the mood is gentle. The pool kindly waives the entrance fees for swimmers, and a wonderful, young, professional swimming instructor – let's call her Tania – volunteers her time to teach those who'd like assistance. Wearing a rashie, goggles and a toothy smile, Tania has a knack for making everyone who comes into the water with her feel secure and cared for.

Tania adeptly tailors each session to the requests and needs of the group. One woman ('G') in the group comes for the benefits of cardiovascular exercise, so Tania has developed a simple program of aquarobics for her. Suffering from type 2 diabetes, G has seen a significant fall in her blood glucose levels and a big improvement in her general health since coming to the pool. Another woman, the mother of two young children, simply comes to relax in the water. Knowing that her two sons are supervised as they play with floating toys, she can switch off, stretch out, float freely and allow the water to wash away some of the day's stresses. A third swimmer has never set foot in the water before, yet by the end of her first class with Tania, she has her face in the water and is blowing bubbles, giggling as she splashes and kicks.

Not long before I attended my first of several classes with this swimming group, I'd watched the SBS drama series *Safe Harbour*. Cleverly contrasting the lives of two groups (five urban Australians holidaying on a yacht, and a group of asylum seekers on an overcrowded, clapped-out boat), the drama uses their encounter in the Timor Sea to throw up a series of moral dilemmas. One vignette from the series stayed with me. After settling into a new life in Australia, an Iraqi boy from the asylum seekers' boat is obliged to attend a school swimming carnival. Aside from the usual apprehensions about body image and acceptance that teenagers understandably bring to such an event, this boy also carries the scars of a waterborne tragedy. A cocky peer's insensitive response to the Iraqi boy's water phobia is to push him into the pool. The Iraqi boy survives the bullying, but it's likely that he will need many more years to recover from his past waterborne trauma.

Happily, Tania's kindness and calmness in the swimming pool counters such indifference and aggression. Enveloping her swimmers with rapport and compassion, she offers them an emotional safe harbour.

37
BEYOND BLUE

IAN THORPE AQUATIC CENTRE, ULTIMO

There's no doubt that swimming is good for you. Anyone who has come out of the water with a heart pumping and a freshly produced dose of endorphins knows the sense of wellbeing that comes from a vigorous swim. Apart from literally getting one's heart racing, swimming builds endurance and strength, tones muscles and can stimulate the production of white blood cells, which in turn can improve overall immunity. Want to counter lethargy, jetlag or a hangover? Then jump in the water and get moving. It's even been suggested that regular swimming can keep you 20 years younger than your chronological age.

Swimming directly improves cognitive health, and research suggests that it can make you smarter, happier and more able to remember things. Clinical psychiatrist Richard A Friedman, writing in *The New York Times*, notes that swimming increases the level of BDNF, a protein that promotes the creation of new neurons in the brain. Immersion in water up to the level of the heart also seems to improve blood flow to the brain, perhaps because of the water's pressure on the chest cavity. Many of my best ideas come to me while I am swimming.

For many of us, water is fundamentally comforting. It's no coincidence that a hot bath is universally seen as a remedy to a tough day. Is our love of water a hardwired link to the memory of being in utero? Or is it that water simply dulls the sensory information that our minds and bodies are usually bombarded with? Whenever I've had an important business meeting, a first date or a job interview, I've always preceded it with a swim. Early-morning swims kept me attentive, fortified and resilient when I sat on the jury of a particularly confronting murder trial, and while staying with my partner on the Northern Beaches during the pandemic, all-season swims in local rock pools kept anxiety at bay. I'm convinced that it was the percolating mental benefits of a swim earlier today that helped me to sort out the logic and structure of this chapter.

There are certainly emotional benefits to swimming, and to that end a pool has constructively figured in my love life. I've done laps as I've imagined a romantic future with the object of a new infatuation, and I swam back to a state of emotional wellbeing after a significant break-up. After moving overseas to be with my German partner, a Bauhaus pool in east Berlin gave me some emotional equanimity as I adjusted to a new home, a new language, and the short, dark days of my first long European winter.

Swimming helped me with the lingering grief that came with the death of my parents. Soon after the death of my father, while I was no doubt still feeling a strong sense of shock, a swim with my eldest brother breathed a semblance of order and meaning back into our jagged selves. The grief I felt with my mother's death was a very different sensation. Over many years, she slowly faded away as Alzheimer's hollowed out her vitality, her speech and her memories. When she died, my brothers and I felt an overwhelming sense of relief, but a knot of grief lodged itself deeply in my solar plexus. Regular swimming seemed to unloose the knot, until one day, without announcement, it simply disappeared.

In the 1993 film *Three Colours: Blue*, a pool is the main venue of therapy for Juliette Binoche's emotionally damaged character, Julie. Near-catatonic from the sudden death of her husband and child in a car crash, Julie gradually processes and accepts her grief as she sobbingly traverses a swimming pool. Saturated in blues, the visual palette of the film mirrors Julie's inner state as she seeks and gains liberty from her grief in the swimming pool.

The Sydney pool that I most strongly associate with mental health is the Ian Thorpe Aquatic Centre in Ultimo. Its namesake became a world champion at 15, broke 23 world records, and won nine Olympic medals. In his 2012 auto-biography *This Is Me*, 'Thorpedo' publicly disclosed that during the peak of his teenage success, he had battled depression, contemplated suicide and had problems with binge drinking. Thorpe acknowledged that there were days when his depression prevented him from getting out of bed. He has poignantly said that his greatest happiness came from simply gliding through the water.

Recovering from those darker times, he has forged a post-swimming career as a broadcaster, philanthropist and champion of social issues. In a 2014 television interview, he came out as gay, and in 2017 he publicly supported the campaign for marriage equality. He has used his considerable celebrity to shine a spotlight on bullying, speak out on the mental health issues that affect elite athletes, and advocate for better health for First Nations Australians.

It is a happy fact that the pool bearing Thorpe's name exudes a sense of therapeutic calm and wellbeing. All white curves and smooth surfaces, the Ian Thorpe Aquatic Centre feels more like a Central European spa than a public pool. It was the last building designed by the Australian Viennese modernist Harry Seidler and, for me, it is one of Seidler's greatest works. Its most striking architectural feature is a giant white ribbed roof. Punctuated with four ribbons of skylight, the roof resembles a huge wave cresting over the main pool before crashing onto Harris Street. Two frosted-glass walls at the north and south ends let in natural light, but, like steamed walls in a shower recess, they also blur the urban harshness of high-rise apartments and a freeway. The western and eastern walls, by contrast, are clear glass and communicate strongly with the city outside. One wall looks out to pedestrians, cars and a row of trees; the other wall opens onto a terrace with dramatic views of the Sydney skyline. Architecture critic Elizabeth Farrelly rated the centre one of the five best buildings in Sydney, calling it 'one of the most enchanting pavilions in the country'.

The water of the main pool is a soothing, pale, glacial blue, and this further adds to the pool's overwhelming sense of tranquillity and wellness. Its hue and glassy surface make me feel like I could be in the lake of a polar cavern. Traversing its 50 metres multiple times, I begin to feel the happiness that Ian Thorpe spoke of – the joy of simply gliding. I feel like my body and the water are one, and on a wet, grey, wintry day, otherwise ripe for melancholy, I truly feel beyond blue.

38
CAN TOO!

BONDI ICEBERGS POOL

Like the world-famous beach that spreads out magnificently to its left, the Bondi Icebergs ocean pool is valorised with superlatives: 'Is there a more photographed pool in Australia?', 'Australia's most iconic swimming club', 'Hard to find a better view in Sydney', 'An international landmark'.

The hype is true. As if passing the Girl from Ipanema, I tingle with delight and go 'aaah' whenever I walk by the pool's turquoise lanes of rippling seawater. I've audibly sighed as I've watched the ocean froth around its icing-white perimeters, and I endlessly enjoy watching the choreography of its swimmers, horizontally aligned like table-soccer players and moving rhythmically back and forth.

Bondi Icebergs on a sunny day is shorthand for all that is most desirable about living in Sydney. Performing the ultimate expression of 'lifestyle', its swimmers sensuously traverse vitreous aquamarine waters then recline on the pool's edges to soak up the rays, and to see and be seen. Glowing with good health after their laps, regular swimmers reward themselves with a sauna, some jovial banter and a coffee, or ascend to the rooftop bar where cool tunes are spun and cocktails are sipped as the sky turns gold and indigo.

But there's more to this pool than lotus-eating. The Icebergs is best known for its famed winter swimming club: every Sunday, from May to September, the club's members take to its waters. For decades, much to the media's delight, the beginning of the winter season has been commemorated by tossing large blocks of ice into the pool. To become (and remain) an Icebergs' member, swimmers must swim three Sundays out of four, in every month over winter, for five consecutive years. Like at a borstal or a strict convent school, rules at the Icebergs are unambiguous and rigidly enforced. Failure to turn up for the required Sunday swims without a written explanation is a breach of the club's Historic Rule 15B and results in a letter of suspension.

I love swimming at the Icebergs in summer but I'm sufficiently self-aware to know that I lack the discipline to ever be an Iceberg. Nonetheless, I'm determined to clock up at least one winter swim here this year.

It's an overcast Sunday afternoon in August, and while the air and sea temperatures are a uniform 16 degrees, the wind whipping off the sea makes things feel downright cold. The swell crashing over the pool's eastern edge is making me queasy and the shivering swimmers I see scurrying from the water look like they're survivors from that famous ship that struck an iceberg. Thinking of Dante's Circles of Hell, I decree to myself that there are at least nine good reasons why I don't want to get wet today. If I were left to my own devices, I'd happily seek refuge in the pool's cafe, but having agreed to meet and swim with a veteran Iceberg, I'm obliged to strip down and take the plunge. My Virgil for today's winter initiation is N, a woman in her sixties who has been an Iceberg for 25 years, lives locally and is a cancer survivor.

Long before I've even shed a pullover, N has stripped down to a one-piece and a swim cap. Inspired by her fortitude and enthusiasm, I begin to peel off layers, but when I eventually don board shorts, a long-sleeved rashie and two swim caps, I feel like a complete fraud. N informs me that there are two approaches to winter swimming. One is to slowly immerse oneself in the pool, step by step, and allow the body to get acquainted with the cold water's whispers of sensation. This is her approach. It strikes me as mindful and disciplined. The other approach, which I embrace, is to simply dive in. Slamming into the sea is both exhilarating and gasp-inducing. I feel the water slap my face below the swim caps and then spread its cold grip along my body all the way to my toes. Moving into a brisk freestyle, I feel as I've been launched into an urgent motion. After about six or seven laps I begin to feel the swim viscerally and start to shiver uncontrollably. As a personal badge of honour, I resolve to swim ten laps in total, then I scamper out of the pool. Stinging from the cold, I huddle under my beach towel with teeth chattering and knees knocking. N, in contrast, swims with a measured and regular stroke for two dozen laps and exits with the same grace that characterised the beginning of her swim.

N tells me that she uses her breathing as her insulating armour. She says that if you can slow the breath and relax into the colder water, it can actually become enjoyable. Controlled breathing not only quietens the brain and the nervous system's responses to the cold, but also generates dopamine and serotonin, which induce positive feelings and emotions. Hormones such as endorphins, adrenaline and cortisol are also released when receptors under our skin are activated by cold water, so the combination of mindful breathing and August water temperatures can be immensely therapeutic. As the coda to her treatise on the virtues of winter ocean swims, N tells me that she believes that frequent exposure to cold water enhances her immune system.

I can't but be impressed by N's strength of body and

spirit, and her generosity. Having survived breast cancer, she embraces winter swimming as a celebration of her recovery and a way of helping others. As well as being a loyal and much loved Iceberg, she swims with the group Can Too, a charity that trains people to undertake physical challenges such as marathons or ocean swims. In return for the training, Can Too participants raise funds for cancer research. N has swum a number of Can Too ocean swims, and in the process has raised thousands of dollars. She speaks passionately of Can Too's philosophy of fun, fitness, friends and fundraising. As she towels off from her Icebergs swim today, she tells me that taking care of herself is important, but so is making a difference in others' lives.

N's goodwill and passion echo the attitude of Sarah Thomas, an American cancer survivor and the first person to ever swim the English Channel four times without stopping. When asked how she felt just before she began her astonishing feat, Thomas's modest response was, 'Am I 100%? No. But I'm the best that I can be right now … with more fire and fight than ever.'

39

GOLD, SILVER, BRONZE

SYDNEY OLYMPIC PARK AQUATIC CENTRE

When we hear the words 'Olympics' and 'swimming' uttered in the same phrase, we swoon as a nation. Swimming is Australia's most successful Olympic sport and its overall haul of medals in the pool since 1900 is second only to the United States. The first time an Australian man and woman ever competed in an Olympic swimming event, gold medals were won, and the tradition of exceptional individual and team results has continued for a century and a quarter.

The first few days of the Olympic Games are keenly watched by Australians because that's when the swimming events are scheduled, and when we usually garner the most of our medals. Sometimes, as in Rio in 2016, the swimming events unfold with 'anticipointment' – when, after much promised glory, the results don't live up to the hype. At other times, such as during the 2000 Sydney Olympics, Australia's results in the pool far exceed our wildest dreams. The men's 4 × 100 metres freestyle relay final on the first evening of competition was the stuff of legend. Anchored by Ian Thorpe, the Australian team broke the world record and ended an American stranglehold on the event that had lasted nine Olympiads.

The other great 2000 moment at the Sydney Olympic Park Aquatic Centre, and one I was lucky enough to see in person, was the men's 1500 metres freestyle final. Like hundreds of others poolside and millions who watched on TV, my brother Mike and I screamed ourselves hoarse as Grant Hackett and Kieren Perkins battled it out for gold and silver. There was something gloriously parochial about the race as it became a two-way Aussie grudge contest, and like teenagers barracking for the champion swimmers in their house teams at a high school swimming carnival, the highly partisan spectators cheered so loud I thought the pool's immaculately designed canopy would collapse.

I think about that fabulous night as I return to the Sydney Olympic Park Aquatic Centre pool 20-odd years later. I've come today with my friend J to swim in the same lanes where Hackett and Perkins duelled. When president of the International Olympic Committee, Juan Antonio Samaranch, first saw the Sydney Olympic Aquatic Centre, he exclaimed that it was 'the best Olympic pool facility' he had ever seen in his life. The Philip Cox-designed pool is indisputably magnificent and it has aged well: its lanes are ice blue, its tiles sparkle under lighting chosen for global broadcasting, and its starting blocks still bear the word 'Sydney' and look like launch pads for drones. Rows of spectator seating keep vigil over the pool, and I think of locals filling them during the Games to wave boxing kangaroo flags and yell 'Aussie Aussie Aussie! Oi oi oi!'

Since J and I both can't decide who will be Grant Hackett and who will be Kieren Perkins, we end up tossing a coin. We laugh as we take our spots on the aerodynamic starting blocks, and prepare for a contest that the nation will be transfixed by: two middle-aged men in Speedos acting like eight-year-olds. We decide that the swim must be 1500 metres – nothing less, nothing more.

Just before we plunge into the water to an imaginary starter's pistol, we size each other up and brag that only one of us can win gold and records will be smashed. Indeed, 14 world records and 38 Olympic records were set in this pool. Then we're in and swimming to glory. Alternately breathing and chuckling as I see J pull faces and surge ahead, I ponder the language of competitive swimming. Why is it all couched in the idiom of violence and plunder? Records are broken, titles are stolen, times are slashed and the competition is murdered. We celebrate killer swimmers who can hammer the field, crush the pack and knock 'em dead. I wonder how spectators (another word suffused with gladiatorial connotations) would react if we spoke of swimming achievement with metaphors of renewal rather than destruction. A champion could regenerate a record, out-bloom the other swimmers and revitalise an event. By the time I've finished my musings, I realise that J has well and truly 'out-bloomed' me.

The Sydney Olympics were a golden fortnight and a template for what a magnificent city Sydney could be. Transport ran smoothly and people used trains rather than cars, the streets hummed with buskers and laughter and international bonhomie, and new building projects gleamed all over the city. Everyone who attended an event, or was glued to the television broadcasts, or just enjoyed Roy and HG taking the piss, had a favourite Olympics swimming memory. I always smile when I think of Eric the Eel. Eric Moussambani is from Equatorial Guinea, which was making its official Olympic debut in swimming. Moussambani had learned to swim in a lake eight months before the Games and had never swum in an Olympic-sized pool until he came to Sydney. He competed in the 100 metres freestyle heat as a wild-card entrant, was the only swimmer in the pool because the other swimmers had made false starts, and was cheered wildly as he finished the race and became a media sensation.

More than two decades after the Games, I think about its legacy as I splash and kick in the jewel of its infrastructure crown. Unlike the nearby stadium and other venues, the pool hasn't been scaled back, repurposed or torn down to make way for apartment complexes of dubious construction quality. After the world's swimming elite left Homebush Bay, the pool was given back to the people of Western Sydney.

Swimmers from 150 nations competed in events at the 2000 Sydney Olympic Games, and Sydneysiders from as many countries have likely swum here in the last 20-plus years. As the suburb now known as Sydney Olympic Park grows in population, its aquatic centre is a much loved and much used recreational meeting place. Some swimmers come here regularly, while for some newcomers, like Eric the Eel, this may be their first experience of an Olympic-sized pool. All these swimmers represent things more precious than gold, silver or bronze: cultural diversity, an enjoyment of the water, and an eagerness to be with family and friends.

SPRING

40
COOK AND OIL
BRIGHTON-LE-SANDS BEACH

This afternoon, I marvel at the indestructible beauty of Brighton-Le-Sands on the western shores of Botany Bay. The bone-white sands of Brighton's long beach glitter like angel dust. Tiny particles of crushed shell sparkle in the spring light and, as if seasoned with herbs, the beach is strewn with needles from a long row of resilient Norfolk Island pine trees. Yet all around the bay, the less-than-desirable impacts of humans undermine its natural assets. Paddle-pop sticks and cigarette butts mingle with the pine needles, and a beautiful vista of distant headlands and rippling teal waves is tainted by the silhouettes of cargo cranes and the Kurnell fuel import terminal.

Botany Bay has had a history of dispossession, controversy, promise and disappointment. Synonymous with Captain James Cook, who, on 28 April 1770, declared Australia 'terra nullius', the bay was subsequently exploited for agriculture, housing, manufacturing, gambling, transport and recreation.

Brighton-Le-Sands was named after the English seaside town of Brighton and, as is often the case with coastal developers in Sydney, avaricious landowners had grand but failed designs. The coast was briefly developed as a seaside resort for weekend holiday makers, but the depressions of the 1890s and 1930s brought poverty and unemployment that lingered until oil refineries were established, and the Sydney airport and Port Botany facilities were expanded.

The beach and environs have been successively abused and scarred by industry and poor planning, bifurcated by heavy traffic and subjected to the frantic roars of aviation. In a city with an embarrassment of coastal riches, the appealing natural corniche of Brighton-Le-Sands was long dismissed by many as simply an undesirable place. Were this bay in another large city (Melbourne immediately springs to mind), Brighton-Le-Sands would be a beloved and much used recreational hub. But rather than celebrate Brighton, Sydney has often fouled its waters with industrial waste. Until relatively recently, oil spills were not uncommon, and many Sydneysiders who were dubious of its water quality justifiably approached Botany Bay with caution.

Happily, the kind of oil that is most associated with Brighton-Le-Sands nowadays is olive oil. Since the 1950s, the area has been home to a large Greek community; many of the cafes and restaurants around nearby Grand Parade serve Greek cuisine and are frequented by residents with Greek heritage. Appropriately, Glyfada in southern Athens is a sister city of Bayside, the municipality of Brighton-Le-Sands. Despite the heavy traffic of Brighton-Le-Sands, people like to dine outside, and the restaurants give evenings here an intergenerational buzz that is lacking on the strips of many of Sydney's beaches. After a swim, it's always a pleasure to dip pita bread in luscious tarama, savour plump olives and briny feta, or treat myself to a strong coffee and some sweet lukumades.

A few years ago, I decided to go to Greece to take stock of things after my mother died. Travelling solo, I walked in the mountains, swam in the Aegean, and spent quiet nights reading myths and spending time in reflection. With each day, I felt my body unclench and my mind clear. I began to sleep well, shed the physical symptoms of grief that I'd harboured in my body and nourish a new sense of calm and wellbeing. I also came to learn of thalassotherapy – the use of seawater as a form of therapy.

In Greek, *thalassa* means 'sea'. The therapy associated with this word involves the systematic use of salt water, littoral climate and sea products to treat specific ailments and encourage overall wellness. The therapy gained its biggest following in Belle Époque France and Victorian England. Like spa towns in Middle Europe, thalassotherapy resorts on both sides of the English Channel offered medicinal bathing. Adherents of the therapy believe that the trace elements of salt water can heal various maladies, and patients are encouraged to take warm seawater showers, and apply mud and seaweed wraps. In Greece, therapies nowadays are less formalised and older people on the coast, particularly women, intentionally bathe in the sea and apply kelp or weed to their bodies to cure skin ailments and promote healing. During many early-morning swims in Greece, older ladies were often my only companions, and they would giggle and nod approvingly as they floated on their backs or scuffed themselves with kelp.

At Brighton-Le-Sands today, the water is rich in kelp. Not having slept well the night before, I feel drained as I stand on the beach and watch the small breakers roll in and out. My fatigue is dispelled as I step into the cold surf of early spring. The cool waves slap my thighs and I hesitate. Either I can retreat and just enjoy the sun and coastal breeze, or I can commit to the waters. I dive deep and when I surface, I gasp with shock at the coldness of the currents. I determine that the only way to remain in the water for more than a couple of minutes is to move quickly and find distraction. As I stroke through the kelp, I feel its slimy limbs reach out and embrace me, as if it wants me to stay. Rather than swim away from the kelp, I frolic among it and find myself bemused. I'm among aquatic friends, and the garden of sea plants – like the Greek people I remember from my travels – insists on being hospitable and caring. Surrendering to this generosity, I forget that the water is cold, and chuckle and splash with abandon.

As I swim in the open sea, I grudgingly acknowledge the beach's small, netted swimming enclosure some way off. I remember coming to Brighton-Le-Sands Baths as a boy with family on Sunday afternoons. My brothers and I would ride the ripples of Botany Bay on our inflated canvas surf mats, and throw jellyfish and huge bunches of seaweed at each other. Like Watsons Bay, Murray Rose Pool, and Clifton Gardens in Chowder Bay, Brighton's baths were surrounded by a grand elevated wooden boardwalk from which kids would maniacally leap into the water. In 1977, during a blessing of the water ceremony, a Greek priest threw a crucifix into the sea and 50 eager believers dived from the boardwalk to retrieve it. Until its dismantling in 1979, Brighton's boardwalk was a place of fun and high jinks, and in a nostalgic protest, I feel disinclined to swim in its shrunken, tethered, pole-less and pier-less replacement. My disappointment in today's less-than-grand enclosure, rather than the cold water, threatens to bring my swim to a premature close, but then a Brighton-Le-Sands memory resurfaces.

Sunday afternoon boyhood swims at Brighton-Le-Sands were often abruptly ended by the imperative to get home, shower off and be at Mass by 6 pm. One Sunday, as we protested our parents' pleas to get out of the water, my eldest, then-18-year-old brother Steve reminded me of a macabre story that an aged nun had told him when he was in infants school. The nun's parable recounted a naughty boy who, like us, had a penchant for leaping off piers and disobeying his parents when they pleaded for him to get out of the water. The boy's mother told the boy that he absolutely had to come in because the family would be late for Mass if he dawdled. Ignoring his mother's pious request, the wilful little boy resolved to have one more jump from the pier. When the boy leaped off, a hungry shark was waiting below, and the boy landed right in the shark's open mouth. The shark had its dinner, the family missed Mass and the boy went straight to Hell.

41
AS SHE TOLD ME

MCIVER'S LADIES BATHS, COOGEE

For decades, female swimming friends have sung the praises of McIver's Ladies Baths. A housemate claimed it as her favourite place in Sydney, a former colleague swam here daily, and a lesbian friend loved the freedom and simplicity of its rustic environment.

McIver's Ladies Baths is a tidally fed pool that sits on a sandstone platform between the Pacific and a soaring cliff. The pool is essentially a naturally formed, 20-metre rock pool. It is entered via a steep and winding path from Grant Reserve, and the circuitous approach plus the dense vegetation, fencing and cliff face that enclose the pool ensure it is a place of great seclusion. It's somewhere that I will never get to see or swim in, and I am happy about this. The women I know who swim here speak uniformly of the baths' cultural significance as a safe, private and welcoming women-only space where they can swim without scrutiny or fear. They strongly advocate for its continued gender-segregated status. Unlike every other swim that I've described in this book, this chapter relies entirely on the accounts of my female swimming friends.

Since European occupation, women have swum continuously at McIver's for almost 150 years, and as the last remaining gender-segregated seawater pool in Australia, it is of significant state and cultural heritage. The baths were dedicated for the exclusive use by women and children in

1876, and were opened on their current site in 1886, but local government documents suggest that colonial women swam here as early as the 1830s. The most I've seen of McIver's is the Colorbond fence that marks the pool's entrance and that bears the sign 'Women and Children Only'. From here, one can also glimpse a wooden rail and steps that descend to the rock pool. As a male, lingering at the entrance feels at best disrespectful and at worst downright creepy.

I ask one of my friends to paint a picture of the baths beyond the entrance and steps. She tells me that what she most loves about the pool is the way it feels organic and naturally hewn. When I ask her to elaborate, she says that the pool nestles in the rock shelf and is embraced by the contours of sandstone that flow like honey. She loves the 'unfinished' quality of the pool and its primitive topography: the rocks that lead into the water are uneven and irregular, the pool's bottom is coarse, and the boulders that sit between the pool and stairway are elemental.

The natural beauty and fabric of the pool, another friend tells me, are equalled by its supportive, unpretentious and friendly atmosphere. Up until relatively recently, she says, admission was 20 cents, collected via an honour system and dropped into a bucket near the pool's entrance. Today it costs $2.50 but this hike in price doesn't seem to elicit protest. 'It would be a bargain at double the price,' she enthuses. My friend has swum at McIver's since the 1980s and speaks passionately about the pool as a haven for women who may feel uncomfortable bathing in front of men because of body issues, religious practice or unpleasant past experiences. She tells me that she swims with pregnant women, lesbians, nuns, Muslim women, breastfeeding mothers, women baring the marks of domestic violence, elderly women, women who are self-conscious about a disability or recent surgery, and women who, prior to coming here, had never before experienced the joy of immersing themselves in salt water.

A third friend who tells me about the pool's history loves the legacy that decades of women swimming together has created. The first two women to ever win an Olympic gold and silver swimming medal, Fanny Durack and Mina Wylie, were both Sydneysiders. Arguably the two greatest female swimmers of their generation, they swam together at McIver's not long before they were denied official funding to compete at the 1912 Olympics. Undeterred by this setback, they self-funded their travels to Stockholm, where they were victorious. Mina's name graces the Edwardian ocean pool that sits a few hundred metres south of McIver's, and Petersham Pool has been renamed the Fanny Durack Aquatic Centre. Rose McIver was another great local swimmer, and her family ran McIver's Ladies Baths until the Randwick and Coogee Ladies Amateur Swim Club took over the lease on the pool in 1922. Four generations of women bearing the McIver name have swum here.

Despite providing a unique sanctuary to such a broad group of women, the pool's gender segregation has been contested by men at various times. In the 1940s, the Mother Superior of Randwick's Brigidine Convent led a successful opposition to calls to enforce mixed bathing. Fifty years later, local resident Leon Wolk took a complaint to the NSW Anti-Discrimination Board, alleging that the pool's exclusion of men was discriminatory. The board refused his complaint, citing the history of the pool, the high regard in which it is held by various female communities, and the fact that three other nearby rock pools offered mixed bathing. To counter similar future complaints, the NSW government granted McIver's an exemption from the state's Anti-Discrimination Act. Rogue men still occasionally attempt to gatecrash the pool, but female council rangers are on call to ensure they leave, and that female swimmers are not harassed or embarrassed.

McIver's Ladies Baths is undeniably a special and important place for the women of Sydney. Its value is best conveyed by one of my closest friends, who is an extraordinary woman, a poet and a long-time lover of the ocean.

Ocean pool

The walk down sandstone steps is one of gritted sensations: the low buzz of insects, scratch of wild grass; shift of shell particles and sand underfoot. I reach the pool's edge, where deeper sounds of the morning recede, replaced by the surge of small waves over amber sea-fronds, curling and uncurling to their own rhythms. From cold air into colder water takes the courage of a second, and I leave behind all land-bound weight and shape: in this space I am defined by long breaths and the sparkle of salt on skin, the twist and glide of strokes above the refracted world that glints and darts away from my shadow. This is where time is a ripple and shimmer, and I find myself, and begin.

42
THE BACKYARD POOL
ENGADINE

There are more backyard swimming pools per head in Australia than in any other country in the world. More than three million Australians live in a home with a pool or spa, and 16 per cent of them are Sydneysiders, despite the fact that a third of us now live in apartments and land sizes are decreasing. Backyard pools have been long the jewel in the crown of domestic affluence for Sydneysiders. As Australia became more prosperous in the 1980s and 1990s, the number of swimming pools in our backyards grew rapidly, and by the new millennium, pools had become common place in many suburbs.

As a child growing up in 1970s south-west Sydney, in-ground backyard pools were almost mythical. I knew no one who had a pool and when, as a seven-year-old, I was invited with my family to the home of a work acquaintance of my father, the sight of a pool in the backyard literally made me wet myself. Luckily this happened before I got into the pool and was likely also due to the large quantities of lemonade I'd consumed. My anticipation of swimming in the concrete pool quickly eclipsed my shame and, changing into my togs, I leaped into the water in a state of near disbelief.

Before this excursion to a backyard in the eastern suburbs, my only experience of a pool that wasn't a council pool was in the Mutual Pools display pools on Canterbury

Road in Campsie. On early evenings in the summer, my brothers and I would hoist each other (and sometimes our dog Monty) over the fence of the compound to jump into the display pools while traffic roared by. In between laps and bombs, we'd wrestle with the Kreepy Krauly (an automated pool cleaner), pretending it was the Creature from the Black Lagoon. Rather than allowing the poor contraption to do its job of maintaining the pool after hours, we'd pretend to stab it, engage it in underwater crocodile rolls or dramatically hurl it out of the water and onto the lovingly laid pebblecrete that surrounded the display pools. No one passing the display compound seemed to notice, much less mind us, and I often wonder how I would react today if I saw five suburban urchins between the ages of seven and 15 splashing deliriously in corporate private property.

About 15 years after our illicit adventures in the Mutual Pools, my parents got their own backyard pool. In the intervening years, my father's fortunes had mirrored those of the country: in the 1970s, at the time of the global oil shock and high inflation, his business reached its nadir; then, in the mid-1980s, his income, like the newly deregulated national economy, suddenly soared. We moved to a larger home in Engadine that had a Driclad above-ground pool in its backyard. Even though the pool was not much bigger than an oversized spa bath, its novelty was huge and wonderful, especially because in our previous house, the most exciting backyard fixtures had been the choko vine and the incinerator. The pool was a wonky metal barrel lined with royal-blue plastic that smelled of garbage bags, and a rickety ladder gave us access to the water. If more than one person splashed around at a time, a large volume of water would seep out, spilling onto and soon killing the buffalo grass that surrounded the pool. A giant chlorine-dispensing buoy that looked like it might contain a genie floated on the surface and emitted chemicals of such strength that they made our eyes red long after we'd climbed out of the water.

After a few more years, my parents decided to put an in-ground pool into their backyard. I believe that it was the first in the street and I vividly remember seeing half of the street's population watch in awe as a huge crane lifted a prefabricated, kidney-shaped fibreglass structure over the roof of the house and drop it into the backyard. The pool had its own filter, used salt rather than noxious chemicals to regulate hygiene, and appropriately hosted its own Kreepy Krauly. Having outgrown the urge to wrestle or damage the contraption, I nonetheless remained oddly in awe of the way the cleaner took possession of the pool, indifferent to swimmers as it ticked and vibrated along the surfaces. I don't know how much the pool cost my parents, but it certainly wasn't cheap. Their purchase was a significant lifestyle investment, and one that they delighted in until they became older and less able to maintain it. For almost 20 years, their swimming pool became a social focus for intergenerational family gatherings and the frequent venue of splashing grandchildren who graduated from floaties to freestyle. Sadly, in the last few years of my father's life, the pool was neglected and, like a metaphor for aging and loss of life control, it filled with leaves and algae.

When my father died, the pool was resuscitated one last time. My mother, suffering from dementia, was entering a care facility and the family home was being sold. A backyard pool that was as black as tar from neglect was not a strong selling point. My dynamic and big-hearted brother Mike enlisted a local tradie, who miraculously restored the pool to its former sparkling glory. Now two middle-aged men, Mike and I bombed and splashed for old times' sake.

Backyard pools in Sydney represent so much more than recreation. They are monuments to aspiration, affluence, status and idealised family life. A pool similar to that built by my parents would likely cost $40000 or $50000 in today's money. Having a pool also comes with great bureaucratic and emotional costs. Excavation and installation work is expensive and time consuming, fencing and geotechnical specifications require rigorous compliance, and landscaping and maintenance can consume huge amounts of money. The environmental costs of having a pool are also high. Pools can require 22000 to 60000 litres of water, and the energy costs of filtering and heating pools is significant. Like my parents, many older people in Sydney feel burdened by the maintenance required for their underused in-ground pools. Companies that 30 years ago would remove or fill in a dozen pools a year are now removing hundreds of pools annually. Despite these costs, we continue to build and maintain pools, and we continue to love them.

Lolling in the backyard pool of friends today, I ask them if all its cost and maintenance is worth it. Without any hesitation, one of my friends replies as my father likely would have answered. A pool, he says, is 'where we come together. It's our haven away from the madding crowd. It just seems "right" to have a pool.'

43
SHELLS, SNAKES, SURVIVAL
LITTLE CONGWONG BEACH, LA PEROUSE

Sometime in September or October, something magical happens in Sydney. The cool gets warmer, and the environment transforms itself in ways that can't be adequately connoted by the word 'spring'. It's not a time of bunnies, bulbs and first buds. It's a time of violet skies and the electric reds of waratahs and bottlebrush, when flying foxes swirl over Sydney in impossible numbers. Foliage glows, snakes emerge from under sandstone, magpies sing their flute-like song and whales can still be seen heading south. Water temperatures remain bracingly cool, and flathead, snapper, flounder and orange roughy reappear in greater numbers.

Swimming in Little Congwong Beach at La Perouse is a splendid way to enjoy the glories of this season. Fifteen kilometres south of central Sydney, Little Congwong sits within Botany Bay National Park. It is backed by a sandstone headland and native vegetation, and it is alive with birdsong. Its sandy, crescent-shaped beach is sheltered and west facing, but the sun at this time of year is warming rather than searing. The beach's gentle ripples and clear water are perfect for paddling, swimming and snorkelling, and a hundred metres out from the beach, there is a clear view out the heads to whales that might pass by.

For tens of thousands of years, Dharawal-speaking clans camped and swam and practised culture at Congwong. They were nourished by a plentiful supply of fish, engraved art into rock shelves, and collected shells for fishhooks, jewellery and ceremonial objects. Their ancestors continue to live close by, and families in the area can trace their ancestors back to pre-invasion times. Artists such as Esme Timbery collected shells from the beach and used them for intricate, beautiful and provocative artworks. It's been said that naming the area La Perouse (after the French navigator who arrived in the area a few days after Arthur Phillip first landed in 1788) symbolically denied the traditional owners of the land any acknowledgement or claim to their Country. Nonetheless, La Perouse may be the only suburb in Sydney where Indigenous people have had an undisputed, unbroken connection with Country for thousands of years, and it's a place of magnificent survival.

In the early days of colonisation, La Perouse was ignored by the British. Deemed too swampy, the northern headland of Botany Bay was officially closed to settlement in 1812. In the 19th century, La Perouse was used as a quarantine area for smallpox, typhoid and influenza, but in 1883 a different virus took hold: segregation. First Nations people from camps around Sydney Harbour and Botany Bay were forcibly relocated to La Perouse by the Aboriginal Protection Board and, when the area was declared a 'Reserve for the use of Aborigines', First Nations peoples were quarantined from white Australia. Missionaries and curious colonisers wanting to see 'natives' visited, but Aboriginal people were not permitted to venture north into settlements and were locked into their reserve.

The arrival of a tram line to La Perouse in 1902 meant that more daytrippers visited, particularly on weekends, and the Kameygal made and sold souvenirs such as boomerangs and shell-covered objects to tourists. The tradition of Indigenous people creating and selling art in La Perouse continues today with the Blak Markets social enterprise that takes place on nearby Bare Island. The steady stream of sightseers brought a bizarre carnival atmosphere to La Perouse, and the most famous weekend sideshow was a succession of 'Snake Men', or handlers, who displayed poisonous snakes to the crowd and sometimes allowed themselves to be bitten. A resident 'snakey' still stands in a pit at La Perouse on Sundays and shows off taipans, adders and brown snakes to freaked-out onlookers.

The Aboriginal Day of Mourning protest in 1938 was an indication that Aboriginal people in La Perouse and elsewhere were becoming politically active in their resistance to the paternalistic administration. Political change was slow to occur, even after Indigenous soldiers fought in World War II. In the 1950s and 1960s, La Perouse's Aboriginal people remained second-class citizens, working in dirty jobs in the Matraville oil works or as domestic helpers at the nearby Prince Henry Hospital. In the 1970s, the La Perouse Reserve was handed over to the NSW Aboriginal Lands Trust, and later to the La Perouse Local Aboriginal Land Council. Today, one-fifth of La Perouse's population is Indigenous and their continued connection to the land, art and storytelling speaks of immense resilience and proud survival.

On this pristine day, Little Congwong Beach seems like a paradise. Luxuriant nature surrounds the few dozen people who relax on beach towels, bob in the cool water or casually stroll up and down the beach's length. Diversity is evident as people of various ages, races and sexualities share the beach. Some bathers are topless or nude and no one seems fussed, and the relaxed tolerance that gently sits on the beach suggests that the social experiment that is Australia is working smoothly. Yet less than a lifetime ago, the original owners of this land, who for thousands of years swam and walked on the beach as we do today, and accumulated vast amounts of natural and cultural knowledge of its land and waters, weren't counted as Australians.

44

THE FILM SET

PALM BEACH

Since the 1920s, Palm Beach has been a playground for Sydney's elite. Located on a peninsula at the northern extreme of metropolitan Sydney, it is remote, exclusive and quiet, and its community likes it that way. Millionaires and film stars have long had weekenders here, and international celebrities are often spotted holidaying on its famous orange sands. Its geography and infrastructure exclaim an historical privilege. The built environment is in stark contrast to the high-rise density of southern beachside suburbs like Bondi, which originally housed working people. Palm Beach's social entitlement is evident in its low-rise housing and large block sizes, limited commerce, infrequent public transport and protected natural habitat. A running joke about the area is that it's remained low-rise because the property developers all live here.

The rich and famous who claimed this beach as their own a hundred years ago had good bloodlines, professional clout and a penchant for entertaining. They played tennis, posed in the latest beach fashions and drank cocktails in immaculately tended gardens. Not a lot has changed. Nowadays, barefoot beachcombers don expensive polo shirts, wide-brimmed hats and elegant patterned cover-ups; they sip single-origin coffee in the cafe on Beach Road; paddle-board on shimmering water like Polynesian princes, and congregate in heritage members-only clubs with names like 'The Pacific Club' and 'The Cabbage Tree Club'. Palm Beach is Sydney's Hamptons.

Life is easy and pleasant in Palm Beach on this glorious October Sunday afternoon. Despite the perfect conditions, it's surprisingly quiet. This is likely due to the 45-kilometre commute from Wynyard, which takes an hour and a half. The trip requires a good bladder and a serious time commitment. Even with your own wheels (and if you're prepared to pay $40 for a day's parking), you're not likely to pop into 'Palmy' for a quick dip. Bounded by the Pacific in the east, Pittwater in the west and Broken Bay in the north, the beach is marooned on an urban dead end, and there's no way of continuing up to the Central Coast by road. You're either here for a well-planned day, or you live here.

The contours of the Barrenjoey Peninsula have always reminded me of a hammerhead shark, swimming out to Broken Bay. If the peninsula is a hammerhead, then Palm Beach is the shark's right flank. Its sands arch from the historic lighthouse of Barrenjoey Head to an Olympic-sized rock pool. The northern end of the beach is choppy while the south is calm, clear and teeming with small fish. Beach Road, the village's main ocean-fronting street, is lined with giant Norfolk Island pines, some 20 metres high and several metres wide. The sand and water are entirely free of litter. Rising upwards from the sand to the spine of the peninsula are architect-designed homes with ancient frangipani trees, sensitively planted native gardens and driveways adorned with BMWs and Porsches. It feels like a movie backdrop for a film or TV series about a coastal idyll. And it is.

For more than 35 years, Palm Beach has doubled as Summer Bay, the fictional setting of the TV program *Home and Away*. The original storyline of the series, which revolved around the travails of five wayward kids fostered by a caring family, had little in common with the privilege or glamour of Palm Beach. Summer Bay was an idealised but unpretentious Everyperson's seaside town and a place where life's dramas were usually resolved with love, good humour and a cup of tea. Over the decades, the series has directly appealed to younger audiences and dealt with themes such bullying, eating disorders, teenage depression and teen pregnancy. Beers, rather than champagne flutes, are raised at Summer Bay celebrations, family dinners tend to be simple and bland, and much of the mostly white cast speak with the inflections of working people.

If *Home and Away* is not reflective of lives truly lived in Palm Beach, the movie *Palm Beach*, which was made by a team including a couple of former Palmy locals, might come a little bit closer to representing the lives of its well-heeled residents. Directed by Rachel Ward and starring Bryan Brown, the film serves up mid-life crisis, infidelity and cancer scares with lots of champagne and fruit platters. Mix in trips to the beach, reminiscences about playing in a band and jokes made at the expense of an aging actress and we have what a *Hollywood Reporter* reviewer called 'a film made by pals in paradise'. Gorgeously shot, the movie nails the intoxicating beauty of Palm Beach. But are the regrets and petty jealousies of wealthy sea-changers the stuff of drama? The French have always made entertaining films about bourgeois malaise and maybe *Palm Beach* is our attempt at this genre, costumed in board shorts and sarongs.

Oscar Wilde famously said that life imitates art and today the beach's reality seems to have taken its cue from the movie *Palm Beach*. Sixtysomething couples and their Gen Y offspring are picnicking extravagantly on the sand. Designer dogs are sentries to locals reading papers and devices. In the rock pool, a smiling, vital, older woman does a personalised program of aquarobics, and beyond the pool, men with granite-hard abdominals paddle-board with poise.

Soon I'm seduced by the beauty and bounty of the beach, and I want to be a part of its glamour and narrative. I walk along the beach with a spring in my step, then I dive into the surf with abandon. Surfacing, I begin to swim like a maniac, as if a film director has just yelled, 'Do it without a care in the world and do it with gusto!' The water is cold, but I realise that I'm smiling. The ocean's tingle and salty kiss are stirring. Wading out of the water I am elated, and I lie on the ochre-tinted sand to dry in the warm sun. Maybe because it's mid-October and the lingering promise of summer outrageously flirts with me, or maybe the fecund, colour-saturated vista mesmerises me, but I feel like a character in a movie that's called *Palm Beach*.

45
SKIN

MAROUBRA BEACH

My first encounter with Maroubra was as a six- or seven-year-old, staying with an aunty who lived a block from the beach. With the hindsight of adulthood, I realise now that she lived in one of the suburb's social housing complexes. Sand seemed to forever blow under her back door, and her red-brick dwelling, though dark, thick-walled and only a couple of hundred metres from the coast, seemed so much hotter than our weatherboard house in Campsie. My aunt's Swedish third husband, a kind and gentle man who was also a periodic alcoholic and prone to benders, worked in a local dairy factory. One of the many novelties of visiting my aunty was eating cereal with cream, rather than milk, and being treated to endless supplies of ice cream. We'd watch the tennis on the black-and-white television, play cards while she drank Reschs Pilsener, and feed their dog Skippa frequent bowls of milk. Visits to the beach were surprisingly infrequent, and I remember smashing bluebottles at the water's edge with my styrofoam kickboard. When I was about ten, my aunt moved interstate and the family ties with the area quickly faded. My memories of Maroubra remained vivid and, while not unpleasant, they did not stoke any adult desires to return.

To my Balmain-centric working-class grandfather, Maroubra was the 'arse end of Sydney'. While my grandfather was not one to mince words, his mid-century perception of Maroubra as less than desirable was widely shared. The stigma attached to Maroubra had its roots in several factors. Maroubra was part of the gazetted La Perouse Aboriginal reserve, and at the end of the 19th century it housed a very large percentage of Sydney's Indigenous population. Many of these First Nations people had been dispossessed from other parts of Sydney and were effectively exiled to Maroubra's dunes and scrubland on the city's fringe. Maroubra was early and potent proof that the colour of one's skin determined where you lived in Sydney (and where you didn't).

Poor and evicted white people on the margins of Sydney's society also made Maroubra home. Unable to pay rent in even the poorest slums, they established squatter camps on the beach, in the caves and along the dunes of Maroubra. At the end of World War II, many of Maroubra's poor were relocated to public housing flats, like the one my aunty lived in. The area's association with social housing likely reinforced negative impressions of Maroubra by increasingly aspirational outsiders, and the proliferation of low-cost housing was resented by developers who saw coastal land as more profitably used for golf courses, private housing, car parks and commercial enterprises. It is interesting that, unlike Bondi or Coogee, Maroubra's beachfront was never comprehensively developed.

In the periods of my adulthood when I was not overseas, I likely accepted prejudices about Maroubra, and instead of returning to a beach of my early boyhood, I adopted Bondi, Coogee and Bronte as my go-to eastern beaches.

In the late 1990s or early 2000s, while working in Hong Kong, I read a piece about the Bra Boys. It was interested to learn that several of the highly territorial surfing gang had grown up in the area's public housing flats and regarded themselves as the beach's racial bouncers. Many of the members have tattooed 'My brother's keeper' across the skin of their chests, and '2035', the postcode of Maroubra, on their backs. Like the Southern Cross tattoos sported by some members of the 2015 Cronulla Riots, the Bra Boys' inked skin speaks of an aggressive parochialism and a highly visible expression of 'Us' and 'Them'. It seems that, like many young men who embrace tribalism as an expression of agency or belonging, the Bra Boys were themselves disadvantaged and excluded. The fact that their fraternity embraced a rhetoric of racial exclusion strikes me as both sad and ironic, particularly because they so vehemently claim ownership of a beach that was for many years home to the city's most marginalised.

I find it hard to reconcile the Bra Boys' fervent tribalism with my many relaxed and happy experiences of Maroubra. In the last decade, I've adopted Maroubra wholeheartedly and often swim here. I love the green southern headland and the sparkling rock pools below it. I love the space and freedom afforded by the long stretch of sand and the undeveloped grassy dunes, which seem to stretch forever. I love clambering over the giant Rubik's Cube at the northern end of the beach, and dispensing and receiving smiles as I walk the beach's length. At the bogey hole on the beach's south, couples – skin to skin – bathe and canoodle romantically, and toddlers smeared in sunscreen squeal with delight as they splash in their parents' arms.

Maroubra strikes me as Sydney's most culturally diverse surf beach. It feels like a beach for all people, all races, all classes, all backgrounds. On this mid-spring Sunday afternoon, it is a beach made beautiful by skins of all colours. Indigenous kids, Polynesian mates, Chinese uni students, women bathing in hijabs and French families attached to the local Lycée Condorcet all calmly and affably share its sand and waves. Skin is bare and often artfully tattooed, or covered by rashies or modest clothing. As we bob together in the sea or share dumping breakers into the shoreline, it seems impossible to square the tribalism of the Bra Boys with what seems like such effortless and cohesive diversity. Yet as a white man with time to come to the beach, I'm not the best person to judge whether all skins are treated equally. Just because I don't personally witness or experience racial slurs doesn't mean that they don't occur, and I wonder what daily life challenges many of my swimming companions might encounter after they leave the surf.

On the day that I came to complete this piece, I engaged in a WhatsApp exchange with one of my closest friends, who now lives in Melbourne. We often call each other 'hermano'. He is someone who has felt first-hand, persistent, 'low-grade' racism and racial glass ceilings, and today he was exasperated by people's attitude to race. During our exchange, he mused, 'Why can't we just love all, and serve all?' I leave the last word with you, hermano.

46
WE CAN BE HEROES

OBELISK BEACH, SYDNEY HARBOUR NATIONAL PARK

As I approach the crisp, clear water of Sydney Harbour on an October afternoon, my naked gay brethren cluster in groups on the sand behind me. I savour the afternoon's easy sensuality as I swim a few brisk lengths of Obelisk Beach, Sydney's pre-eminent gay beach. Returning to the sand and to my friend T, I imagine that the phalanx of sunbathers, arranged in formations of friendship groups, is a heroic army from antiquity, ready to defend the values of freedom, pleasure and pride.

Obelisk sits within the Sydney Harbour National Park, between Middle Head and Georges Head. It is one of Sydney Harbour's official 'clothing optional' beaches. Its sister nude beach, Lady Bay, sits directly across the harbour. It's a beautiful place where all men, regardless of their age, ethnicity, body type or identity, can meet and socialise without judgement, fear or harassment.

Before homosexuality was decriminalised and gay men could legally meet in bars and nightclubs, beaches and the harbour had been clandestine meeting places or 'beats' for many years. In his superb book *Gay Sydney: A history*, Garry Wotherspoon recounts how the Bondi Pavilion and Giles Baths in Coogee were famous beats in the first half of the 20th century. Decades earlier, and at a time when sodomy was still a capital offence, men seeking sex with other men would meet at the Domain Baths, Sydney's first free public swimming baths. Fittingly, these saltwater baths were in the section of the harbour that would later be occupied by the Andrew 'Boy' Charlton Pool, arguably Sydney's most gay-friendly swimming pool.

Meeting at beaches or by the harbour was not without its dangers. Other than the convictions, blackmail and entrapment that frequently occurred until homosexuality was decriminalised in New South Wales in 1984, gay men were often subjected to violence and 'poofter bashing', and several gay men were murdered at beaches and on cliffside coastal beats. Many of these crimes remain unsolved, suggesting, at best, a police reluctance to investigate and prosecute gay-hate crimes.

The value of beautiful places like Obelisk for gay men to meet openly, relax safely and socialise without victimisation or vilification cannot be underestimated. The right to gather publicly without fear or intimidation is something that past generations of gay men in Sydney were never able to enjoy, and the activists who lobbied for gay legal reform are true and brave heroes.

Spaces like Obelisk allow us to drop our guards as well as out kit. When one is in one's birthday suit, there's literally nowhere to hide. I've found that whenever I've stripped bare on Obelisk, I've often engaged in open-hearted and revealing conversations. Perhaps being nude in a natural setting helps us to be more childlike and dispense with social prohibitions, or perhaps fully revealing our bodies helps us to more fully disclose our inner selves.

I notice that a sunbathing neighbour is reading *Haunt of the Black Masseur*, Charles Sprawson's sprawling celebration of the swimmer as hero. The book is marvellously apt for today. Sprawson's book gives an account of how swimming has meshed with literature and culture since the classical age, and argues that gay men have been central subjects in this narrative. From the classically besotted uranianists of Victorian times to the jubilantly naked divers in David Hockney's swimming pool paintings, gay men have been key figures in the nexus between swimming and heroic art. A gay sensibility is similarly apparent in Australian art and literature inspired by swimming. Works such as Max Dupain's homoerotic photograph *Sunbaker* and Christos Tsiolkas's novels *Barracuda* and *7½* are clear examples. The sight of Sprawson's book prompts me to ask T what it means to be 'heroic'. For a delightful second, I ask myself if we would be having this conversation if we were fully clothed.

Our conversation follows a few destinations before arriving at the first Mardi Gras, which we both regard as a seminal and heroic act of civil disobedience. In the almost 50 years of parades since the arrests of 1978, Queer people have championed their rights to be heard, included, and treated with equality and dignity. Wrapping iron fists in sequined gloves, parade entrants have protested, marched, danced and shimmied for social change.

Recalling memorable past parades, my friend and I remember the final float a few years back. Representing Amnesty International's 'Rainbow Amnesty' group, the marchers held placards with beautiful faces and tragic captions: a gay youth murdered in Chechnya, a Brazilian LGBTQIA+ activist executed. Hovering over these sad stories was a gigantic banner that spoke of solidarity and authentic heroism. It read, 'Together we can all be brave.'

47
THE SUPERSTAR
BONDI BEACH

Patrick White wrote about it, Brett Whiteley painted it, Midnight Oil sang about it, Heath Ledger acted on it. Ladies and gentlemen, I give you … Bondi Beach.

Bondi is an unruly coastal circus and that's why I love it. If I wasn't from Sydney and had ties to other parts of the city, I would, as many new arrivals and backpackers have done, adopt Bondi as 'my Sydney'. I guess I can with some legitimacy claim Bondi as part of who I am. My parents grew up not far from each other and both were walking distance from Bondi's golden crescent of beach. Like many postwar Australians, they moved from Art Deco flats in the eastern suburbs into larger, freestanding homes in new outer suburbs, but Mum and Dad continued to talk fondly about growing up in Bondi and about the 'Bondi Broad' – a much-loved cousin who steadfastly refused to budge.

Undoubtedly Sydney's most famous beach, Bondi is a coastal superstar. The history of Bondi largely mirrors the history of Sydney and much of its story feeds our national narratives.

For thousands of years the Bidjigal, Birrabirragal and Gadigal peoples have lived on and around the beach, and their rock engravings are still very visible in the area. In the early days of colonisation, Bondi was largely covered in sand dunes. Pastoralists who had purchased the Bondi area tried their hand at grazing cows where skateboarders and spray-painting street artists now congregate. Bondi was re-acquired by the state as a public beach in 1882 and, following Federation, the archetype of the bronzed, male, Anglo Bondi Lifesaver was elevated to almost mythic status. Like the Digger and the Swagman, the Bondi Lifesaver came to represent 'Australia' in advertising, wartime propaganda and jingoistic conversations about class, gender and race.

In the 1920s, 1930s and 1940s, Bondi typified conflicts between those wanting to conserve and those wanting to commercialise Sydney's beach life. User-pay change rooms; an organised opposition to a giant, never-to-be-realised amusement park; real estate booms and busts; and erratic 'beautification' programs were chapters in this struggle.

During World War II, the beach was heavily fortified in case of Japanese invasion, but people found their way past barbed wire and littoral defence blocks to swim at the beach. Soldiers keeping vigil slept in the tunnels that run under Campbell Parade and, ironically, the few men of service age who could be found on the beach during the early 1940s were American servicemen visiting Sydney on 'rest and recreation' leave.

Peace, as well as war, left its mark on Bondi Beach, and in a brilliantly orchestrated royal photo opportunity, a newly crowned 27-year-old Queen Elizabeth II famously traversed the beach in the back of a jeep. In the years following the war, large immigrant populations moved to Bondi, forever transforming the tone and flavour of the area, and setting the scene for today's cultural diversity. Bondi's giant car parks spoke of a newly mobile suburbia, and its Central European cake shops, Greek milk bars, Jewish delis and emergent backpacker culture pointed to a changing Australia.

Bondi has long been associated with skin and sin. In the great Australian novel *The Tree of Man*, Nobel Laureate Patrick White called it a place of 'many furtive lusts'. By the 1980s, Bondi's reputation for hedonism and unlawful behaviour was widely known. Peter Corris, who has been referred to as 'the Godfather of contemporary Australian crime-writing', portrayed Bondi as a place of drugs, decay and sleaze. Bondi was also infamous for violent, unsolved gay-hate crimes.

Like much of Sydney, Bondi got a makeover for the 2000 Olympic Games and, despite local protests, it hosted the beach volleyball events. Property prices soared with the arrival of the new millennium, and young corporate movers and shakers such as the Packers and Murdochs moved in, building or renovating multimillion-dollar beach pads. Marketing itself as a haunt of affluence and celebrity, Bondi once again reinvented itself.

One of the most appealing aspects of a visit to this beach is encountering its many tribes. Dreadlocked Brazilians, power walkers, frolicking Nippers, gay boys, hippie girls, influencers, car hoons and paddling Chinese tourists are as at home at Bondi as the early-morning, all-year surfers and the leathery long-time locals. Billed as the world's biggest fun run, the City2Surf ends at Bondi every August. As it brings the smell of Dencorub and 70000 joggers down the hill from Dover Heights and onto the beach's finish line, this avalanche of diverse humanity easily melds with the regular, colourful Sunday morning Bondi crowd.

'Bondi' is one of the few place names that has firmly entered the popular lexicon of Sydney. A local will immediately collocate it with 'Icebergs', the famous ocean pool, but older Sydneysiders will also likely pair 'Bondi' with the word 'tram'. The expression 'shoot through like a Bondi tram' is one of coastal Sydney's most endearing idioms, bested only perhaps by a phrase my grandfather used to describe a male weakling: 'He's got a Bondi chest!' – that is, far from Manly! My grandfather, an ironically vain and self-deprecating man, would sometimes admire himself in the mirror. Combing his still considerable volume of septuagenarian hair, he'd joke, 'You won't see better waves than those at Bondi.'

The word 'Bondi' is derived from a Dharawal word meaning 'loud thud', and it refers to water breaking over rocks. At the northern end of the beach, waves wash over the rocks with the impact and self-possession of a superstar, and this is where I most love to come to swim when I'm at Bondi. Stroking out beyond the Mermaid Baths towards Flat Rock and leaving the colourful seaside circus behind me, I arrive at verdant sea gardens that are teeming with dazzling fish and intriguing sea creatures. Pipefish, seahorses, anemones and tube worms weave in and out of kelp and algae, and sea urchins, limpets and periwinkles cling to the tidally massaged shoreline. It's miraculous that the waters of this most famous of beaches are so abundantly alive and varied, and, like its extraordinary history and the diverse human cavalcade on the water's edge, this is cause for adulation, cheering and applause.

48
AWAY FROM HER
SOUTH CRONULLA ROCK POOL

I have very different and sometimes very conflicting memories when I visit Cronulla. When I was a child who lived in south-west Sydney in the 1970s, Cronulla was a happy day at the beach that involved bodysurfing with my brothers, watching my father and mother visibly relax, and eating freshly deep-fried potato scallops. I have an unforgettable image of my father lying on the sand with his front torso to the sun, an oversized grin on his face, and his closed eyes covered by two tissues scrunched into protective balls. A few years later, when my family moved to southern Sydney, Cronulla seemed more complicated as I negotiated the culture shock of going from a multicultural high school where many of the kids' families had escaped war or terror in Lebanon, to a school where most of the kids were Anglo-Celtic and underage drinkers.

Perhaps more than any other beach in Sydney, Cronulla is freighted with associations other than sand and surf. Cronulla is Sydney's longest beach, and Kamay Botany Bay National Park lies at its northern end. This is close to where Captain Cook first landed in 1770; to the Gweagal people, the beach's traditional owners, and other First Nations Australians, it is the 'ground zero' of British occupation. Cronulla is also the only city beach that can be visited by rail and, as a result, it is more directly accessible and more contested than many other beaches in Sydney.

Many older white Cronulla residents celebrate the fact that Captain Cook made his first landing in the (Sutherland) Shire and that they live in the 'birthplace of a nation'. Many of Cronulla's locals are similarly proud of the remembrance that they give to sons who died on the battlefields of Europe last century. A large and beautifully landscaped war memorial has pride of place between the beach and the railway station. An old-timer at the beach once fondly reminded me that *Forty Thousand Horseman,* the epic Charles Chauvel film about the Australian Light Horse of World War I, was filmed on the beach's sand dunes.

A friend and Shire resident once likened the Shire to Sydney's version of pre-1989 West Berlin – it is happily inward-looking and self-contained, fiercely territorial and sus-picious of neighbouring areas – particularly the less affluent, more multicultural suburbs of south-west Sydney. The racial tribalism that had long existed between those who live near the beach and those who don't came to a toxic head on 11 December 2005. On this day, groups of local men brandishing Australian flags and inked with Southern Cross tattoos screamed slogans like 'We grew here, you flew here', and clashed with groups of Lebanese men. I was living overseas when the Cronulla Riots happened, but I sometimes wonder whether any of the people who were engaged in the riots were the children of people that I went to school with in Marrickville or in Cronulla.

Not long after the riots, my father died, my mother was diagnosed with Alzheimer's, and I moved back to Australia. My mother had moved into a care home in the Sutherland Shire, and despite growing forgetfulness and confusion, she was still very physically agile. As a treat which we'd both enjoy, I'd take her swimming in the South Cronulla Rock

Pool. My mother was described by a gerontologist as being 'delightfully demented', meaning that she did not suffer from the aggression or confusion that can often beset people with Alzheimer's. She was as meek and compliant as a lamb on Prozac, so there was never any resistance or drama when an outing to the rock pool was suggested. Up until her final years, Mum maintained a sense of fun that was central to her personality, and it was wonderful to be able to engage this by going swimming together.

The benefits of aerobic exercise to brain health have been widely documented, but researchers increasingly believe that aquatic exercise can greatly improve the health and wellbeing of people living with dementia. Aside from the normal cardiovascular and postural-strengthening benefits of swimming, water therapy can improve balance and motor coordination. These aspects of health are often attacked by dementia, and sufferers are more prone to falls and stumbles than other elderly people. A 2014 Queensland study suggested water-based exercise can give dementia sufferers a sense of purpose, elevate their mood, and trigger long-term happy memories. These benefits, plus a strong sense of stress-free, shared fun, are things that I remember from my swims with Mum in the rock pool.

The South Cronulla Rock Pool is built on a sandstone platform between the beaches of north and south Cronulla. It is easily accessed, so getting there on a regular weekday was never a problem. An accessibility ramp into the water and a mostly regular waist high depth meant that Mum and other elderly people could enter, exit and enjoy the water safely. Once in the water, we mostly played. I would hold Mum's hands and pull her along and we'd make jokes about tugboats and crocodiles. After a swim, we'd have an ice cream or fish and chips on the beach and these treats added to our sense of wellbeing. Mum would often smile and say, 'I remember coming here.' Perhaps she did, or perhaps as dementia experts note, Mum's use of the words 'I remember' was more an expression of feeling secure, rather than truly recalling. Regardless, swimming gave us something to share that wasn't complicated, was framed by nature, and was sensual and invigorating. It also gave Mum happy pause from her sometimes very perplexing life in an institution.

I found that on the days we swam together, I also became more relaxed. In the same way that bath time with small children is a shared pleasure for parents and children alike, I found that swimming with Mum, bobbing together in the water and splashing playfully gave us a joy removed from many of the day's confusions.

Not long after my mother was diagnosed with Alzheimer's, I saw the film *Away From Her*. In the movie, Julie Christie plays a physically vital woman who is diagnosed with Alzheimer's and who moves into a care home. After the move, she begins to lose all memory of her still-living and supportive husband, and begins a relationship with another man. The storyline, and Julie Christie's performance, were remarkably poignant for me, particularly as Mum began to fade away from her old self and lose track of people who'd once been intensely important to her. The film also made me realise that ultimately memories are never objective, and – depending on who does the remembering – they are endlessly contestable.

Sadly, over time, Mum's physical state deteriorated with her mental health, and our outings to the beach came to an end. For her last two years of life, she was like a swaddled babe, smiling, innocent and entirely dependent on others for her most basic care.

Exiting Cronulla railway station today, I pass the grand World War I memorial and I feel discomfited by the fact that there are seven memorials in the Shire to soldiers who fought and died on foreign soil, but none to the frontier wars that began close by. I'm also surprised by the flood of boyhood and adolescent memories that come to me as I stroll towards the beach. I've come to Cronulla to visit a great friend of Mum and Dad's – a vital and delightful octogenarian – and to swim in Mum's honour in the rock pool. Remembering this, I try to put aside bigger memories and just think of my mother, because she is what matters today.

In the water of the rock pool, I move like a tugboat, glide like a crocodile, and bob up and down like an infant. A familiar joy embraces me and while I can't deny that I'm away from her, Mum's palpably in my thoughts and memories. After my swim, I sit looking at the gulls and waves and blue sky and, with an ice cream in my hand, I smile and say to myself, 'I remember coming here.'

49
CITY OF JOY

BRONTE BATHS

In her book *Why We Swim*, Bonnie Tsui suggests that we are compelled to take to the water for five reasons: survival, wellbeing, community, competition and flow. I would add that we also swim to find a state of joy.

Joy differs from wellbeing in that it is both a disposition and a distinct emotion. It's a uniquely pleasant and positive state, yet it can be shared with other emotions (such as elation, happiness, and even sorrow). *The Oxford Companion to Emotion and the Affective Sciences* argues that joy 'feels bright and light. Colours seem more vivid. Physical movements become more fluid. Smiles become difficult to suppress. Joy broadens people's attention and thinking.' If this explanation is accurate, Sydney swimming may be at its most joyful in November at Bronte Baths.

November in Sydney heralds many reasons to feel joyous. Daylight saving has arrived, days are markedly longer, and skies are violet to complement the jacarandas and agapanthus that are in riotous full bloom. Ocean temperatures are warming up, the mania of December's 'silly season' is still some way off, and the stupor of January is even further in the future. Media outlets broadcast information other than cricket scores, and humidity levels in November are a fraction of those to come in February and March. The heady scent of star jasmine filters into open windows as those glorious blossoms spill over wooden fences and climb up verandahs. Mosquitoes have yet to mount their summer campaign. Mangoes have arrived.

On this cloudless November Friday afternoon, Bronte Baths feels supremely light and bright. The baths have a near-perfect easterly aspect, and as the sun hits the waves that ripple through the baths, it creates mesmerising, dancing patterns. As I swim through the water, I'm delighted by the networks of intricate sunrays. It looks like a benevolent fairy has generously thrown glitter over the entire pool. In and out of the water, the sunshine feels healing and magical. Even on an overcast day, Bronte Baths is one of the city's prettiest swimming places, but today, as it glistens and sparkles, it is breathtakingly beautiful.

As the water coruscates, colours seem more vivid. Usually when I swim in an ocean pool, I approach the water for a few moments, savour the elements around me and then begin the serious business of doing laps. Today, it seems sacrilegious not to stop frequently and consciously register the bright colours of this perfect day. The ocean beyond the baths is a heady tapestry of teal, turquoise and ultramarine, and the borders of each patch of colour are blurred by subtle tints and shades. The stone perimeter of the baths, a warm marble-pink, is the same colour as the sand of the beach 50 metres away. Patches of moss green carpet the bottom of the pool and complement the colours of Bronte's grassy northern headland.

It's joyous to see an abundance of bright colour in and under the water. Swimmers' cossies are wildly patterned and luridly coloured: fluoro pink, baby blue, lime green. The waves that rinse the baths clean with each new high tide deliver fish and sea creatures into the swimming lanes, and today my companions are baitfish, toadfish and some small but eye-catching yellow-and-black fish. I have yet to encounter another city in the world that offers Sydney's experience of free public swimming in an animated, natural, tidal aquarium. As I register the colours and details of this underwater fairyland, I smile broadly.

Despite the frequent breaks between laps to enjoy the light and colour, my physical movements have become more fluid on this joyous Bronte afternoon. Joy might be the reason for this. Or maybe it's because Bronte Baths is only 30 metres long, so I'm swimming shorter laps. I like the pool's heritage wooden turning board that divides the serious 30-metre lap swimmers from the kids in floaties. It gives an order to this unpatrolled, self-regulated pool.

The baths are one of Sydney's grand old ocean pools and they have an illustrious history of fluid movement. They were built in 1887, and the 'Australian Crawl' (better known as the 'freestyle' stroke) was introduced to the world here in 1901 by a Solomon Islander named Alick Wickham. Bronte Baths was an early hotspot for Australian competitive swimming and among the greats to take the plunge into its venerable, algae-dusted lanes was Fanny Durack, Olympic champion, and the world's greatest female swimmer from 1910 to 1918. The Bronte Splashers (descended from the Waverley Amateur Swimming Club) is among the oldest swimming clubs in the world and, 130 years after the Waverley club's formation, the Splashers continue to meet every Sunday morning, welcoming one and all. Happily, the swim club no longer ends its proceedings with a duck hunt, as they did in 1890.

In a joyful state, smiles become difficult to suppress and at Bronte today, there are plenty of reasons to beam. For surfers, there's a great swell; for vitamin D–loving gourmands, there are alfresco cafes; for the kiddies, there's a protected ocean bogey hole and a miniature train; and for picnickers, dogs and ball enthusiasts, there's a fabulous verdant park.

Joy broadens people's attention and thinking. When the baths opened in 1887, they applied strict rules of gender segregation: ladies could swim between 10 am and 4 pm Monday to Saturday, and outside these hours and on Sundays, the pool was for gents only. Today, the bathing citizenry is diverse in gender, age, ethnicity, sexuality and swimming experience, and the baths are open 24 hours a day. The pool is free, it's regularly cleaned, and the swimmers who adore it scrupulously maintain its care and beauty.

As I loll with fellow swimmers in the cooling public waters of Bronte baths and we enjoy its pleasures, we smile, we talk, and we relax like epicurean Romans. And, like Romans, we realise that we enjoy tremendous luck and privilege. I feel that this aquatic meeting place is something enormously precious: an intersection of nature, history, culture and community, and I *know* that my sense of joy ever relies on such intersections.

50

'THE SWAMP'

LAWSON SWIM CENTRE, UPPER BLUE MOUNTAINS

The world has just recorded its hottest year ever and entered what the United Nations Secretary-General called an 'era of global boiling'. While Sydney has been spared the carnage of bushfires for several years, fires have ravaged other parts of the country. Across northern and north-west Australia, 610 000 square kilometres burned – an area of devastation bigger than entire countries such as Spain and Thailand. Terrifyingly, the fires extended into the wet tropics and into arid areas that, previously, had enjoyed a long and successful history of Indigenous cultural fire management. I hadn't tuned into the full severity of the northern Australian fires until I received a visit from my friend E, who lives in the Territory.

I'm on the way to Wentworth Falls with E to visit a mutual friend. As we climb the mountains, he explains to me that above-average dry-season temperatures in the Top End, and increased vegetation encouraged by the rains of past La Niña events, had fuelled fires that had lasted for several months. Some of these fires came close to Darwin and Alice Springs.

En route, we've decided to stop at the Lawson Swim Centre for a quick swim before dinner. The train chugs with festive bonhomie. It's Friday mid-afternoon and everyone ensconced on the train's padded purple seats knows that after we ascend a few hundred metres the reward will be fresh air, pristine bushland and a leisurely weekend. Given the nature of our conversation, it seems ironic that the swimming pool we're headed for indirectly owes its existence to the railway and to plumes of black smoke. When steam train services across the Blue Mountains began in 1867, reliable water supplies were used to keep the trains running. There was a natural lake in Glenbrook in the lower mountains but, after that, dams needed to be built along the way.

Christmas Swamp and its marshy grasslands was the first area to be dammed, and Blue Mountains Station was built here. Trains in both directions stopped at Christmas Swamp to take in water, and to make the place sound more salubrious, the dam was renamed 'Lawson'. When a bigger dam was built at Wentworth Falls and the swamp was no longer needed, Lawson's dam was transformed into a natural swimming pool. For 40 years, residents swam among the gum trees until an open-air Olympic pool was built on its site. Nowadays the pool is nicknamed 'the swamp'.

Alighting at Lawson station, the air is fragrant and sweet. I was once told by an Armenian scientist that the perfect microclimate for good health is an altitude between 500 and 1000 metres. I have no idea if this is true. Maybe the scientist shared this fact because it squared with the environment in which he happily lived. Escaping the sea levels of busy Sydney for the immaculate environment of elevated Lawson, and shellshocked by details of the fires in the Top End, E and I are 100 per cent convinced the scientist is right.

With fresh air stoking a sense of wellbeing, we amble the short distance from Lawson station to the pool. So far this season, fire has bypassed the Blue Mountains, but the bush here is tinder dry and I pray that it remains unscathed.

A corner of Lawson dam was nicknamed 'Snakey Gully' and since a local friend has told me snakes also commute along the path from the station, we show due respect for our reptile friends, avoid the long grass and keep to the paved road.

At the pool's entrance, we count out some coins for the entrance fee and exchange hellos with the friendly young attendant. The infrastructure of Lawson Swim Centre is not dissimilar to many pools constructed in the 1960s. Its red-brick change rooms are modest, and its canopy-covered plastic picnic tables host simple pleasures. It's a friendly, unpretentious and tranquil place. The pool is surrounded by bushland, and this setting is what makes a swim here sublime and unique. Fringed by gum trees, visited by flies and animated by the songs of cockatoos and whipbirds, the pool feels more like a billabong than a municipal pool. A few slender leaves lie on the bottom of the pool like eucalyptus bêche-de-mer.

Our dive into its water is utterly cleansing. With every lap of the bush-encircled pool, we feel as if the din and congestion of the city we left just two hours ago is further and further away. The swim feels particularly invigorating for E who, not that long ago, was choking on the pall of fires and going stir-crazy with the imperative to stay inside. He tells me that the swim has helped to wash the fires of out of his pores and his spirit. Pristine and transforming, this pool is the antithesis of a swamp.

After the swim, we hop back on the train to enjoy a weekend with a dear friend in Wentworth Falls. Over dinner, this friend is also eager to hear details of the Top End fires and we listen attentively as E provides further details. As he speaks, I feel as if everything has been weirdly inverted, as if in a twisted fairy tale. Clouds from bushfires envelope the tropical Top End, but the sky above Lawson's bushland is deep blue and benign, and the 'swamp' is sparkling. It seems a perverse reversal of the natural order that someone from the tropics should seek relief from bushfires in the Blue Mountains.

I voice this incongruity, and E frowns and nods. We ask each other: 'Is this what climate change looks like?'

51
THE UNDERWATER BUSHWALK
GORDONS BAY

The mental and physical health benefits of walking in the bush or forest have long been documented. In *Losing Eden*, British writer Lucy Jones extols the countless daily virtues of green space. We know that even in cities, pedestrians instinctively track walking paths that follow trees and detour from treeless streets. What's less known is that contact with underwater plants and habitat may also have several health benefits. Apart from the circulatory benefits that are associated with swimming in water that is highly oxygenated by aquatic plants, there is strong anecdotal evidence to suggest that contact with seaweeds and seagrasses may nourish the body, remediate some skin diseases, and ease aches and pains. Whenever I snorkel among seagrasses or marine gardens, I also feel a sense of emotional wellbeing. Aquatic plants attract marine animals, remove carbon from the water, and animate underwater habitats with colour and movement. After a snorkel in a rich and green aquatic reserve, I feel like I've had an underwater bushwalk.

Gordons Bay sits between Coogee and Clovelly beaches and is part of the Bronte-Coogee Aquatic Reserve. It can only be accessed by foot, but since it's right in the middle of the Bondi to Coogee cliff walk, it's hardly a well-kept secret. Sitting between two large cliff faces, the bay's setting is dramatic and the bushland that surrounds it is diverse in plant, bird and animal life. The waters' many aquatic species can be wonderfully interpreted thanks to informative underwater signage. Like a bushwalk in a national park, the Gordons Bay Underwater Nature Trail is a self-guided adventure trail, but one for scuba divers and snorkellers. The 600-metre trail consists of 25 concrete-filled drums that are 20 metres apart and linked by a chain. Steel plaques display information about the marine and plant life in the bay and by following the chain, divers can safely complete the trail and see a wealth of clearly identified marine life.

Sharks, rays, invertebrates and scores of fish species call the bay home. Gordons Bay is also habitat for sponges, kelp and seagrasses. The usually calm conditions of the bay mean that underwater vegetation thrives. Healthy vegetation brings marine life, and healthy marine life brings enchanted divers and snorkellers.

My friend T and I share several interests. We're both seasoned travellers, we're inveterate nature lovers and we relish novelty. Since we like to bushwalk and swim, we can't resist the opportunity to enjoy both interests simultaneously at the Underwater Nature Trail. It's Friday afternoon and, while the late-November water is still a bit chilly, the chance to cool off after a hot and tiring day is welcome. The soft light that arcs into the bay and the clear shallow water that diffuses it are seductive. We acknowledge the luxury of living in a city where one can end the working week with a snorkel. Happy and excitable, we pull on fins and spit in our masks.

Within seconds of plunging under the water's cool surface, we enter a dreamy realm of colour, choreography and hierarchy. Coastal fish, schooling fish and bottom-dwelling fish vie for our attention, and we smile and point as we swim among them. Bulbous red rock cod look like cranky cussing elders, while schools of pomfret resemble phalanxes of armoured Spartans. Beardies bring to mind beatnik poets, and the pop-eyed roughy looks like a demented raver whose pill has just kicked in. I'm always struck by the individual and vivid personalities of fish whenever I snorkel, and I am surprised that it took several decades of animation before a film like *Finding Nemo* finally hit the screens. Like any rich marine habitat, Gordons Bay is its own universe of characters and storylines.

After frolicking among the fish in the algae and rock shelves, we find the first drum of the trail and follow its chain into deeper water. Port Jackson sharks and wobbegongs are common in Gordons Bay and while we don't see either today, we spot a mottled stingaree on the seabed. I see its tail before I make out its eyes and initially it looks like a flattened porcupine. Once I orientate myself to its front, it resembles a stealth bomber. The underwater trail takes about 40 minutes to complete, but since we've already seen a lot of fish and I'm starting to shiver, I decide to swim back in. Close to the shore, I'm treated to an encounter with a couple of blue gropers. They're huge and iridescent, and their giant fleshy faces and pursed lips are almost sensuous.

I surface close to where we entered the water and, looking at my phone as I towel off, I'm surprised to see we've been under the water for almost half an hour. Time gallops underwater, and I remember when I did a scuba-diving course many years ago, our instructor earnestly warned us of this potential danger. Despite the cool temperature of the water, I feel immensely relaxed, almost as if I've just had a long bath. Certainly, the beauty and animation of the marine life has calmed and delighted me, and though I've been breathing through a snorkel, my lungs feel clear and expanded. Seagrasses are believed to sequester carbon from the atmosphere in the same ways that forests filter the air and capture carbon to build their trunks. Perhaps the air above this aquatic reserve of seagrass also has cleansing and restorative properties.

As I wait for T to surface, I take in the bay and its beauty. Like an unexpected lookout discovered midway in a long bushwalk, the view is a gift that deserves pause and wonder. We walk in our bushland and along our coast to escape the pressures and doubts of modern existence and to feel regenerated. When we are stressed or in need of a reset, we walk among forests, flowers and shrubs. The pandemic taught us anew that time in green and blue space was essential to good mental health, and that the sea, like trees, can revive us. By surrendering ourselves to the familiar yet mysterious embrace of the element that most defines our city, we can feel whole again. Tingling with salt and watching the kelp ripple under the water, I feel completely satisfied. After half an hour at Gordons Bay, I feel as if I've just completed a challenging but magnificent bushwalk.

SUMMER

52
MINA AND JOANA
WYLIE'S BATHS, COOGEE

Unlike a good parent or an impartial teacher, I have a favourite. Wylie's Baths is not only the grand old dame of Sydney's ocean pools and my favourite Sydney swim, it's also my favourite swimming venue in the entire world. A note to future mourners – this is where I'd like a good portion of my ashes to be scattered. But more about that later.

I've started many a swimming season in Wylie's chilly September water, farewelled languorous summers with a dip in May or June, and sometimes, unable to wait till the next spring, have come back in winter with a wetsuit. I've greeted numerous underwater sea creatures as I've traversed the pool's 45 metres and habitually chatted to other biped regulars who float and swim and giggle. I've resisted the urge to stalk celebrities who love the pool as much as I do and, upholding the democracy that only Speedos can bestow, have instead offered, and received, a nod and a smile.

After a swim, I've bought many a flat white and slab of carrot cake from the pool's tuckshop. The humble shack has steadfastly resisted culinary gentrification and sells oversized refrigerated rolls that make my jaw hurt when I bite them. In every season and weather condition imaginable, I've looked out from the sublimely sited heritage-listed deck that sits on wooden stilts above the rock pool. Taking in Wedding Cake Island and the churning Pacific, I've never failed to swoon, and with each visit I reaffirm to myself and various companions that there is no better view in the world.

I've delighted in the change rooms that are grafted onto the curves of honey-coloured sandstone and feel like a stage set from *South Pacific*. Lit by cheerful skylights, aired by sea breezes and made of simple plywood, the change rooms host hot solar-powered showers that need a 20-cent coin to be activated. On days when the ocean is cold enough to make me shiver uncontrollably after ten laps, these showers have thawed and soothed me.

I've patted the pool's resident pussy cat, listened to seagulls that squawk and swoop for fish offshore, and read numerous books in the shady hollows beneath the deck. I've taken my turn with other regulars scooping bluebottles out of the pool in late summer, and I've marvelled at the blue groper who blithely swam with us for weeks. I've enjoyed the festive colour and geometry of beach towels spread elaborately on the large cement sundeck, and, as if holding coveted tickets to a gala performance, I've tailored entire itineraries of visiting family and friends around a swim here. I've heralded several Christmas mornings with a Wylie's swim and a mango on the Edwardian boardwalk, and I've been repeatedly charmed by the pool's annual ritual of enshrining a decorated Christmas tree in the very middle of the water.

Today, I realise that I've clocked up my 52nd swim for the year. I'm reminded of what a glorious time Sydney in December can be. If the year is a working week and summer its weekend, early December is the equivalent of 3 pm on a Friday: the best is yet to come and it's tantalisingly close.

Walking through a grove of banksias and hearing the swell of the sea, I skip towards the entrance to the pool, a shack of vertical blue-and-yellow stripes that evokes bathing pavilions of bygone days. Descending to the entrance gate, I happily note that the water temperature is 20 degrees and I ripple with excitement at my first glimpse of the pool in several months. I proffer a handful of coins to gain entry. It's a magical and fair swap – a handful of gold and silver for an hour of aquatic perfection. If I had them in my pocket, I'd also offer sapphires, emeralds and jade in homage to the colours of the sea.

Wylie's Baths is one of Sydney's oldest ocean pools, established in 1907 by Henry Alexander Wylie, a local resident and celebrated swimmer. Wylie's daughter Wilhemina (better known as Mina) learned to swim here; she and her friend Fanny Durack went on to become the world's first female swimmers to win silver and gold medals at the Olympic Games. An endearing bronze statue of Mina Wylie in a neck-to-knee bathing suit welcomes visitors to the Baths. Every time I come to Wylie's, I give Mina a friendly wink. She seems to enjoy the view to the Tasman from her vantage point among beds of frangipani and kangaroo paws.

Mina Wylie is not the only remarkable female local who I associate with Wylie's. For many years until she died before her time of 'an unlucky tumour', I swam regularly at Wylie's with my friend Joana. A New York native but a child of the world, Joana enthusiastically adopted Coogee after lives in Brooklyn, Perth, Central Australia and Samoa. Having worked as a health educator in Iraq, Liberia, Papua New Guinea, China and South-East Asia, Joana told me that the only thing that got her more excited than an aquatic 'appointment with Dr Wylie' was a travel tale. Brassy and sassy, she used language as salty as Wylie's water. She revelled in referring to a senior government minister as a 'passionless c$#t' and would conduct hilarious, impromptu poolside vox pops with other swimmers. Joana had a quirky sense of humour and would often end text messages with pseudonyms that referenced contemporary culture. When *The Handmaid's Tale* television series premiered, she was 'Offred'; when a famous prisoner was released from a Bali gaol, she was 'Schapelle'. If nothing in the news or of the zeitgeist amused her, Joana would often sign off a message as 'Mina'. It was therefore entirely appropriate that Joana's wake was held at Wylie's, and that her ashes were scattered close by.

On the day that Joana's closest friends came to send her to the seas, I thought about why many of us (including me) want our mortal remains to be given to water. An essential and healing element, its embrace is both familiar and mysterious. We are predominantly composed of water and its absence is literally life-erasing. Like our city, our island nation and our fragile blue planet, our bodies depend on water. Our need for water is also emotional – without it we are less free to escape the pressures and doubts of modern life. Swimming can be an initiation, a meditation, an act of liberation. The routines, physical ebbs and flows, and surprises of a swim parallel our individual journeys as life's emotional tides rise and fall. A swim can wash away past setbacks, irrigate hope and cleanse us emotionally.

Swimming is living, and swimming Sydney connects us with Country, ourselves and each other.

NOTES

1 Rites of passage: Shelly Beach, Manly
'home to more than 160 species of fish': New South Wales Department
      of Primary Industries, 'Cabbage Tree Bay Aquatic Reserve map',
      n.d., <www.dpi.nsw.gov.au/content/fisheries/marine-protected-
      areas/aquatic-reserves/cabbage-tree-bay-aquatic-reserve>, accessed
      16 March 2024.
'Near the Fairy Bower car park … large shell midden': NSW Marine Estate
      Management Authority, *Hawkesbury Shelf Marine Bioregion Assessment:
      Review of 15 pre-identified sites*, NSW Department of Industry, Skills
      and Regional Development, Sydney, 2016, p. 30, <www.marine.nsw.
      gov.au/__data/assets/pdf_file/0008/594872/hawkesbury-shelf-pre-
      identified-sites.pdf>, accessed 8 May 2024.

2 Fraternité: Clovelly Beach
'Its regular squares … kept local men in work': Randwick City Council,
      'History of Clovelly', 2023, <www.randwick.nsw.gov.au/about-us/
      history/historic-places/historic-suburbs>, accessed 16 March 2024.
'Clovelly is the largest naturally occurring swimming pool in Sydney':
      Dillon Seitchik-Reardon and Caroline Clements, *Places We Swim:
      Exploring Australia's best beaches, pools, waterfalls, lakes, hot springs and
      gorges*, Hardie Grant, Melbourne, 2018, p. 24.
'used to be called "Little Coogee"': Caroline Ford, *Sydney Beaches: A history*,
      NewSouth, Sydney, 2014, p. 49.
'In 1902 … mixed swimming in daylight hours': Ford, *Sydney Beaches*, p. 49.

3 Moonlight: Mahon Pool, Maroubra
'Like many of Sydney's ocean pools … employment relief program':
      Charlotte Anlezark, 'Heritage ocean pools to visit this summer',
      National Trust (NSW), 20 December 2022, <www.nationaltrust.
      org.au/blog/heritage-ocean-pools-to-visit-this-summer/>, accessed
      16 March 2024.

4 'May you be well …': MacMasters Beach
'Bouddi's national park listing … saved from development': Heather
      Radi, 'Byles, Marie Beuzeville (1900–1979)', *Australian Dictionary of
      Biography*, 1993, <https://adb.anu.edu.au/biography/byles-marie-
      beuzeville-9652/text17027>, accessed 16 March 2024.

5 Ancestors: Nielsen Park and Parsley Bay Reserve, Vaucluse
Kenneth Slessor, 'Five Bells', in *Selected Poems*, HarperCollins Publishers, 2014.
'Also titled Five Bells … sea-harbour is in me"': Art Gallery of New South Wales, 'Five bells, 1963', n.d., <www.artgallery.nsw.gov.au/collection/works/133.1999/#about>, accessed 22 March 2024.
'when Fred Astaire sang to Ginger Rogers … and love and romance"': Lyrics from 'Let's Face the Music and Dance' by Irving Berlin, introduced in the 1936 film *Follow the Fleet*.
'Scott Bevan describes gazing … as a vision"': Scott Bevan, *The Harbour: A city's heart, a country's soul*, Simon & Schuster, Sydney, 2017, p. 426.
'In 2016, the seawall … 100-year-old life': NSW Office of Environment and Heritage, 'Replacement of the Nielsen Park seawall', 2024, <www.environment.nsw.gov.au/topics/parks-reserves-and-protected-areas/park-management/community-engagement/sydney-harbour-national-park/nielsen-park-seawall-rebuild-project>, accessed 16 March 2024.
'Construction of the new seawall … run over schedule': Danuta Kozaki, 'Nielsen Park locals frustrated as reopening of Shark Beach delayed by defects found in rebuilt seawall', ABC News, 4 February 2024, <www.abc.net.au/news/2024-02-04/futher-delays-sydney-nielsen-park-shark-beach-reopen/103423556>, accessed 16 March 2024.
'Not long ago I saw a remarkable … titled *Sea of Memories*': See image at Maggie Steber, <www.maggiesteber.com/main.html>, accessed 16 March 2024.

6 Miracles and ghosts: Giles Baths, Coogee
'Bathing for non-Indigenous men only began … 19th century': Randwick City Council, 'Giles Baths', 2022, <www.randwick.nsw.gov.au/facilities-and-recreation/beaches-and-coast/ocean-pools/giles-baths>, accessed 16 March 2024.
'The baths then became Lloyd's Baths … indulged in"': Ignacio Palacios, *Sydney Rock Pools*, Ignacio Palacios Travel Photography, Sydney, 2014, p. 106.
'Giles' history as a male-only … and 1950s': Palacios, *Sydney Rock Pools*, p. 106. See also Garry Wotherspoon, *Gay Sydney: A history*, NewSouth, Sydney, 2016, pp. 49–50.
'a result of the "Ekman transport" effect': Scott Elias, 'Changes in ocean circulation patterns', in *Threats to the Arctic*, Elsevier, Cambridge, MA, 2021, pp. 27–44.
'In her memoir *Turning* … heroin': Jessica J Lee, *Turning: A swimming memoir*, Virago, London, 2017, p. 178.

10 'Always was, always will be': Victoria Park Pool, Camperdown

'crafted by Kooma man Brett Leavy and the team at Virtual Songlines':
See Virtual Songlines, <www.virtualsonglines.org>, accessed 16 March
2024.

'Victoria Park was originally Blackwattle Creek': Paul Irish and Tamika
Goward, 'Blackwattle Creek', Barani: Sydney's Aboriginal History,
2013, <www.sydneybarani.com.au/sites/blackwattle-creek>, accessed
16 March 2024.

'"Barrenjoey" is said to mean "young kangaroo"': David Tribe, Tracey
Howie, et al., 'Meanings in Guringai Country', Budawa Aboriginal
Signage Group, 2018, <budawagroup.com/meanings-in-guringai-
country/>, accessed 16 March 2024.

'There's conjecture that Parramatta Road … following the pathways of
First Nations people': Sue Daniel, '"Walking in their tracks": How
Sydney's Aboriginal paths shaped the city', ABC News, 17 May 2018,
<www.abc.net.au/news/2018-05-17/curious-sydney-aboriginal-
pathways/9676076>, accessed 16 March 2024.

'It was built in 1953 … to task this requirement': City of Sydney, 'History
of Victoria Park', 27 March 2013, <www.cityofsydney.nsw.gov.au/
histories-local-parks-playgrounds/history-victoria-park>, accessed
16 March 2024.

'The trees that I look at … cheese tree': Mike Macphail, 'A hidden cultural
landscape: Colonial Sydney's plant microfossil record', *Australasian
Historical Archaeology*, vol. 17, 1999, pp. 79–105.

'Yabun festival … Aboriginal and Torres Straits Islander cultures': See Yabun
Festival, <yabun.org.au>, accessed 16 March 2024.

12 Storm clouds: Cockatoo Island

'Cockatoo Island housed a girls' reformatory … were physically maltreated':
Sydney Harbour Federation Trust, 'Schools for girls and boys:
Educational institutions', Cockatoo Island, n.d., <www.cockatooisland.
gov.au/en/learn/island-history/educational-institutions/>, accessed
2 May 2024.

'In 2000, an Aboriginal rights group … clan or family now extinct"': Sydney
Harbour Federation Trust, 'History of Wareamah: First Nations',
Cockatoo Island, n.d., <www.cockatooisland.gov.au/en/learn/island-
history/first-nations/>, accessed 30 May 2024.

13 The Swimming Pool Library: Andrew 'Boy' Charlton Pool, Sydney

'Singer-songwriter Loudon Wainwright III agrees': Loudon Wainwright III,
'The 10 best places to swim in the world, according to me', *New York
Times*, 19 August 2017, <www.nytimes.com/2017/08/19/opinion/
sunday/best-places-swim-world.html>, accessed 16 March 2024.

'Casey Legler … this gorgeous pool': Lyndsey D'Arcangelo, 'Casey Legler opens up about her searing memoir', *Curve*, 4 October 2018, <www.curvemag.com/blog/author-interview/casey-legler-opens-up-about-her-searing-memoir/>, accessed 16 March 2024.

'*New York Times* reviewer Catherine Stimpson … can cherish"': Catherine R Stimpson, 'Not every age has its pleasures', *New York Times*, 8 October 1988, <www.nytimes.com/1988/10/09/books/not-every-age-has-its-pleasures.html>, accessed 16 March 2024.

'bathed in the area, which was called the Fig Tree': City of Sydney, 'Andrew "Boy" Charlton Pool', City of Sydney Archives & History Resources, 2024, <archives.cityofsydney.nsw.gov.au/nodes/view/1724476>, accessed 16 March 2024.

'the largest masters swimming club in New South Wales': Wett Ones Swimming Club, <www.wettones.org>, accessed 16 March 2024.

14 Grandfathers: Watsons Bay

'Australia's greatest shipbuilding and repair program': Australian Senate Standing Committee on Foreign Affairs, Defence and Trade, 'The early years of naval vessel construction and repair in Australia', in *Blue Water Ships: Consolidating past achievements*, Standing Committee on Foreign Affairs, Defence and Trade, December 2006, pp. 39–40.

'In her novel *Seven Poor Men of Sydney*, Christina Stead … transport barges'. Christina Stead, *Seven Poor Men of Sydney* (1934), Angus & Robertson, Sydney, 1987, p. 3.

'journalist Scott Bevan … large holes': Bevan, *The Harbour*, p. 406.

'a German shepherd called Rexie': Tsem Rinpoche, 'Rexie: The Australian heroine', Tsemrinpoche.com, 10 September 2016, <www.tsemrinpoche.com/tsem-tulku-rinpoche/animals-vegetarianism/rexie-the-australian-heroine.html>, accessed 16 March 2024.

15 #shack: Burning Palms, Royal National Park

'In the 1930s … Clontarf': Ford, *Sydney Beaches*, pp. 91–92, 94.

'listed on the New South Wales State Heritage Register in 2012': Erin O'Dwyer, 'Beach heritage shacks of Royal National Park', *Australian Geographic*, 2 November 2012, <www.australiangeographic.com.au/travel/travel-destinations/2012/11/beach-heritage-shacks-of-royal-national-park/>, accessed 16 March 2024.

16 Bare truths: Lady Bay Beach, Sydney Harbour National Park

'Such was the distaste for … in New South Wales': Ford, *Sydney Beaches*, p. 25.

'In 1907 … a "sea kilt"': Madeleine Wedesweiler, 'Compulsory swimming skirts for men almost became law, long before g-string bans', SBS News, 22 February 2024, <www.sbs.com.au/news/the-feed/article/g-

string-bans-arent-new-modesty-laws-once-led-to-men-swimming-in-skirts-at-bondi-beach/c9mflcn12>, accessed 16 March 2024.

'Protesters marched … kitchen curtains': Louis Nowra, *Sydney: A biography*, NewSouth, Sydney, 2022, p. 319.

'a year before American nuclear testing … Sydney beaches': Ford, *Sydney Beaches*, p. 216.

17 The siren: Tamarama Beach

'the beach was transformed by colonial hucksters … 70 turnstiles': Ford, *Sydney Beaches*, pp. 18–19, 35–38.

'With more rescues per 1000 swimmers … patrolled beach in New South Wales': Surf Life Saving Sydney, 'Tamarama', 2014, <surflifesavingsydney.com.au/club-directory/tamarama/>, accessed 16 March 2024.

'Every year, about 100 people drown … victims are local': Royal Life Saving Australia, *National Drowning Report 2023*, Royal Life Saving Australia, Sydney, 2023, <www.royallifesaving.com.au/research-and-policy/drowning-research/national-drowning-reports>, accessed 16 March 2024.

'Professor Rob Brander': For everything there is to know about rips, check out Rob Brander's *Dr Rip's Essential Beach Book*, NewSouth, Sydney, 2023.

'"The Cathedral", from Tim Baker's collection': Tim Baker, 'The Cathedral', in *Out From the Past*, Collins, Sydney, 1988, pp. 125–154.

18 Dawn in April: Dawn Fraser Baths, Balmain

'Australia's oldest existing public swimming pool': Inner West Council, 'History of Dawn Fraser Baths', 2022, <www.innerwest.nsw.gov.au/explore/aquatic-centres/dawn-fraser-baths/about-dawn-fraser-baths/history-of-dawn-fraser-baths>, accessed 17 March 2023.

19 The sacred and the profane: North Curl Curl Rock Pool

'In his novel *Taboo* … granite': Kim Scott, *Taboo*, Pan Macmillan, Sydney, 2017.

20 The children: Mermaid Baths, North Bondi

'Speaking at the installation … climate change issue"': AAP, 'Sea rise set to drown kids' pool', *Sydney Morning Herald*, 16 September 2017, <www.smh.com.au/news/environment/sea-rise-set-to-drown-kids-pool/2007/09/16/1189881342959.html>, accessed 16 March 2024

'According to OzCoasts … moderate scenario': OzCoasts Australian Online Coastal Information, <ozcoasts.org.au/>, accessed 16 March 2024.

'Coastal Risk Australia … the year 2100': See Coastal Risk Australia, <coastalrisk.com.au/home>, accessed 16 March 2024.

'It's been estimated that … $9 billion a year by 2060': Tamsin Rose, 'Natural disasters could cost NSW $9bn a year by 2060, analysis finds', *The Guardian*, 23 February 2024, <www.theguardian.com/australia-news/2024/feb/23/natural-disasters-could-cost-nsw-9bn-a-year-by-2060-analysis-finds>, accessed 16 March 2024.

21 The pen is mightier than the board: Thirroul Pool
'Thirroul features largely … "raving with moonlight"': DH Lawrence, *Kangaroo*, Martin Secker, London, 1923, <www.gutenberg.org/files/59848/59848-h/59848-h.htm>, accessed 16 March 2024.
'*The Railwayman's Wife*': Ashley Hay, *The Railwayman's Wife*, Allen & Unwin, Sydney, 2013.
'Louis Nowra beautifully describes … personally"': Nowra, *Sydney*, p. 495.

22 Puberty Blues: Gunnamatta Bay Baths, Cronulla
'*Puberty Blues*': Kathy Lette and Gabrielle Carey, *Puberty Blues*, McPhee Gribble, Melbourne, 1979.

23 Exile and quarantine: Little Bay Beach
'the Dharawal people … outbreak of bubonic plague': Randwick City Council, *Botany Bay National Park: Heritage Conservation Area*, n.d., <www.randwick.nsw.gov.au/__data/assets/pdf_file/0017/26072/Botany-Bay-National-Park.pdf>, accessed 22 March 2024.
'Caroline Ford documents … eye infections': Ford, *Sydney Beaches*, p. 233.
'created the world's largest artwork': Kaldor Public Art Projects, 'Project 01: Christo and Jeanne Claude', 2024, <kaldorartprojects.org.au/projects/project-1-christo-jeanne-claude/>, accessed 22 March 2024.

24 Our pool: MacCallum Pool, Cremorne Point
'After its initial theft … English-style pleasure garden': North Sydney Council, 'Cremorne Point History Walks'.
'It started as a rock pool … maintain it': 'Hugh MacCallum', *Monument Australia*, Monument Australia, 2010–2024, <monumentaustralia.org.au/themes/people/community/display/90205-hugh-maccallum>, accessed 20 March 2024.
'Called "the C-word" by Tim Winton … little bargaining power"': Tim Winton, 'Using the C-word', in *The Boy Behind the Curtain*, Penguin Random House, Melbourne, 2016, pp. 219, 232. Quotes are reproduced with kind permission of the author.
'the incomes of the top fifth … more than six times': Australian Council of Social Service and UNSW Sydney, 'Inequality in Australia', Poverty & Inequality, n.d., <povertyandinequality.acoss.org.au/inequality/>, accessed 31 May 2024.

25 The Secret River: Brooklyn Baths

'"An Island Life"': James Worner, 'An Island Life', in *Strange Objects Covered with Fur: 2015 UTS Writers' Anthology*, Xoum Publishing, Sydney, 2015, pp. 245–253. Quotes are reproduced with kind permission of the author.

'Kate Grenville describes … its walls of rock and bush"': Kate Grenville, *The Secret River*, Text, Melbourne, 2005, p. 102. Quotes are reproduced with kind permission of the author.

'a repository of significant First Nations cultural sites': NSW National Parks and Wildlife Service, 'Bulgandry Art Site Aboriginal Place: Brisbane Water National Park', 2024, <www.nationalparks.nsw.gov.au/things-to-do/aboriginal-sites/bulgandry-art-site-aboriginal-place>, accessed 16 March 2024.

'In 2013, the little-understood POMS … breeds of oysters': Department of Primary Industry, Fishing and Aquaculture, 'Pacific Oyster Mortality Syndrome (POMS) current situation', 18 April 2013, New South Wales Government, <www.dpi.nsw.gov.au/fishing/aquaculture/info/poms/hawkesbury-river-update>, accessed 16 March 2024.

26 On Golden Pond: Lake Parramatta

'*Wild Swimming*': Sally Tertini and Steve Pollard, *Wild Swimming: Sydney Australia*, Wild Things Publishing, Bath, UK, 2015.

'Lake Minninup … massacred': The Centre for 21st Century Humanities, 'Site list timeline', Colonial Frontier Massacres in Australia, 1788–1930, 2022, <c21ch.newcastle.edu.au/colonialmassacres/timeline.php>, accessed 24 May 2024.

27 Red leaves and Rose: Murray Rose Pool, Double Bay

'Murray Rose has been … individual events': Sport Australia Hall of Fame, 'Murray Rose AM', 2020, <sahof.org.au/hall-of-fame-member/murray-rose/>, accessed 18 March 2024.

'In its obituary … absolutely relaxed"': Richard Goldstein, 'Murray Rose, Australian Olympic swimming star, dies at 73', *New York Times*, 15 April 2012, <www.nytimes.com/2012/04/16/sports/murray-rose-australian-olympic-swimming-star-dies-at-73.html>, accessed 18 March 2024.

'On his Ocean Pools NSW blog … as his togs': Simon Duffin, 'Murray Rose Pool, formerly Redleaf Pool, Double Bay 2028', Ocean Pools NSW, 12 January 2016, <oceanpoolsnsw.net.au/murray-rose-pool-formerly-redleaf-pool-double-bay-2028/>, accessed 18 March 2024.

28 The Golden Girls: Annette Kellerman Aquatic Centre, Marrickville
'mentored by Olympic gold medallist … swimming the mile': Sport
    Australia Hall of Fame, 'Annette Kellerman', 2020, <sahof.org.au/
    hall-of-fame-member/annette-kellerman/>, accessed 18 March 2024.

29 Wild swimming: Glenbrook Gorge, Blue Mountains National Park
'*Wild Swimming* … hemming you in"': Tertini and Pollard, *Wild Swimming*,
    p. 190.

30 The crypt: Cook + Phillip Park Pool, Sydney
'Architect and writer Laura Harding … civic monuments"': Laura Harding,
    'Protocol failure: Sydney's public urbanity is disappearing behind
    aggressive, private individualism', ArchitectureAU, 21 August 2019,
    <architectureau.com/articles/protocol-failure-sydneys-public-
    urbanity-is-disappearing-behind-aggressive-private-individualism/>,
    accessed 18 March 2024.

31 Nobody's gone surfing: North Narrabeen Rock Pool
'*Travelling to Tomorrow*': Yves Rees, *Travelling to Tomorrow*, NewSouth,
    Sydney, 2024.
'The title of "Australia's first surfer" … been surfing at Manly': Australian
    National Surfing Museum, 'Secret surfing history – Isabel Letham',
    27 November 2021, <australiannationalsurfingmuseum.com.au/
    secret-surfing-history-isabel-letham/>, accessed 18 March 2024.
'The oldest known image … wooden board': Australian National
    Surfing Museum, 'Australia's surfing story', 10 January 2020,
    <australiannationalsurfingmuseum.com.au/australias-surfing-
    story/'>, accessed 18 March 2024.
'In his memoir … conventional life': Tim Winton, 'The wait and the flow',
    in *The Boy Behind the Curtain*, pp. 131–132. Quotes are reproduced with
    kind permission of the author.
'The beach's Boardriders Club … in Sydney': Ford, *Sydney Beaches*, p. 203.

33 Wade: Marrinawi Cove, Barangaroo
'just five minutes by the sea can strengthen … mental health': Daniel
    Nutsford et al., 'Residential exposure to visible blue space (but
    not green space) associated with lower psychological distress in a
    capital city', *Health & Place*, vol. 39, May 2016, pp. 70–78, <www.
    sciencedirect.com/science/article/abs/pii/S1353829216300119>,
    accessed 31 May 2024.
'Its namesake … the NSW colony': Place Management NSW,
    'Barangaroo the woman', n.d., <www.barangaroo.com/past-
    present-future/history-of-barangaroo/barangaroo-the-woman>,
    accessed 16 March 2024.

34 Grand design: Prince Alfred Park Pool, Surry Hills
'"Beneath the deluge"': Catherine M Brennan, 'Beneath the deluge',
    in *Beneath the Deluge*, Cinnamon Press, Gwynedd, Wales, 2008.
    Reproduced with kind permission of the author.
'Professor Philip Goad calls … urbanism"': Phillip Goad, 'Prince Alfred
    Park Pool', ArchitectureAU, 17 December 2013, <architectureau.com/
    articles/prince-alfred-park-pool/>, accessed 21 March 2024.
'Before the park was even … ice rink next door': City of Sydney, 'History
    of Prince Alfred Park', 27 March 2013, <www.cityofsydney.nsw.gov.
    au/histories-local-parks-playgrounds/history-prince-alfred-park>,
    accessed 21 March 2024.

35 Swimming with Frankie: Pacific Swim School, Crows Nest
'Babies have instinctive buoyancy skills': Steven Shaw and Armand
    D'Angour, *The Art of Swimming: In a new direction with the Alexander
    Technique*, Ashgrove Publishing, Bath, UK, 1996, pp. 67–68.
'The brain activity … more comfortable than their non-swimming peers':
    Caitlin Boyle, '8 benefits of infant swim time', Healthline, 21 July
    2023, <www.healthline.com/health/parenting/infant-swimming>,
    accessed 21 March 2024.

37 Beyond blue: Ian Thorpe Aquatic Centre, Ultimo
'can stimulate the production of white blood cells': University of Brighton,
    'Is open water swimming good for you?', 10 February 2023, <www.
    brighton.ac.uk/news/2023/is-open-water-swimming-good-for-you>,
    accessed 30 May 2024.
'It's even been suggested … chronological age': K Aleisha Fetters,
    '10 benefits of swimming that will have you diving into the pool',
    Shape, 2 January 2020, <www.shape.com/fitness/workouts/benefits-
    of-swimming>, accessed 21 March 2024.
'Clinical psychiatrist Richard A Friedman … *New York Times*': Richard A
    Friedman, 'Pool of thought', *New York Times*, 16 July 2016, <www.
    nytimes.com/2016/07/17/opinion/sunday/pool-neuroscience.html>,
    accessed 21 March 2024.
'In his 2012 autobiography … through the water': Ian Thorpe, *This Is Me*,
    Simon & Schuster, Sydney, 2012.
'Architecture critic Elizabeth Farrelly … in the country"': Elizabeth
    Farrelly, 'The five best buildings in Sydney', *Sydney Morning Herald*,
    14 November 2013, <www.smh.com.au/national/nsw/the-five-best-
    buildings-in-sydney-20131114-2xijh.html>, accessed 21 March 2024.

38 Can too!: Bondi Icebergs Pool
'"Is there a more photographed pool … international landmark"': See
  Seitchik-Reardon and Clements, *Places We Swim*, p. 20; Bondi Icebergs
  Club, <icebergs.com.au>, accessed 21 March 2024; and Sydney.com,
  'Bondi Icebergs', 2024, <www.sydney.com/destinations/sydney/
  sydney-east/bondi/food-and-drink/bondi-icebergs>, accessed
  21 March 2024.
'Historic Rule 15B': Bondi Icebergs Club, 'Swimming membership',
  <icebergs.com.au/swimming-membership/>, accessed 21 March
  2024.
'Hormones such as endorphins … cold water': Richard A Friedman,
  'Is swimming in cold water good for you?', *Washington
  Post*, 11 September 2023, <www.washingtonpost.com/
  wellness/2023/09/11/cold-water-swimming-depression-mood/>,
  accessed 21 March 2024.
'Controlled breathing … feelings and emotions': Amber Smith, 'The
  benefits of deep breathing', *Upstate Health*, Spring 2020, p. 16,
  <issuu.com/upstate/docs/upstatehealth_covid2020fnl>, accessed
  31 May 2024.
'Thomas's modest response … than ever"': Rachel Elbaum and Caroline
  Radnofsky, 'American cancer survivor is first to swim the English
  Channel four times nonstop', *NBC News*, 17 September 2019, <www.
  nbcnews.com/news/world/american-cancer-survivor-first-swim-
  english-channel-four-times-non-n1055196>, accessed 21 March 2024.

39 Gold, silver, bronze: Sydney Olympic Park Aquatic Centre
'When president of the International Olympic … in his life': Cox
  Architecture, 'Sydney International Aquatic Centre', n.d., <www.
  coxarchitecture.com.au/project/sydney-international-aquatic-
  centre/>, accessed 21 March 2024.

40 Cook and oil: Brighton-Le-Sands Beach
'Adherents of the therapy believes … seaweed wraps': MC Lucchetta et al.,
  'The historical-scientific foundations of thalassotherapy: State of the
  art'. *Clinical Therapeutics, vol.* 158, no. 6, pp. 533–541.

41 As she told me: McIver's Ladies Baths, Coogee
'as the last remaining gender-segregated seawater … cultural heritage':
  Ford, *Sydney Beaches*, p. 282.
'Four generations of women bearing the McIver name have swum here':
  Vincent Rommelaere and Amanda Woods, *Rock Pools of Sydney*, Unseen
  Australia, Sydney, 2021, pp. 146–147.
'In the 1940s, the Mother Superior … mixed bathing'. Palacios, *Sydney Rock
  Pools*, p. 111.

'Leon Wolk … an exemption from the state's Anti-Discrimination Act':
Helen Pitt, 'Martha or Arthur? Cossies in a twist at ladies-only
baths', *Sydney Morning Herald*, 11 December 2010, <www.smh.com.
au/national/nsw/martha-or-arthur-cossies-in-a-twist-at-ladies-only-
baths-20101210-18swq.html>, accessed 25 May 2024.
Catherine M Brennan's 'Ocean Pool' is reproduced with kind permission
of the author.

42 The backyard pool: Engadine

'There are more backyard … any other country in the world': Tim
McIntyre, 'The big myth about home swimming pools', *Daily
Telegraph*, 26 December 2016, <www.realestate.com.au/news/the-big-
myth-about-home-swimming-pools/>, accessed 21 March 2024.
'More than three million Australians … Sydneysiders': 'One-in-seven
Australians (3.1 million) live in a house with a swimming pool or spa',
Roy Morgan, press release, 15 August 2023, <www.roymorgan.com/
findings/9311-australian-swimming-pool-ownership-march-2023>,
accessed 21 March 2024.
'a third of us now live in apartments': Catherine Hanrahan and Tony
Ibrahim, 'Australia's census asked about high-rise living for the first
time – this is what it revealed', ABC News, 29 June 2022, <www.
abc.net.au/news/2022-06-29/census-high-rise-living-data-reveals-
sydney-is-national-hot-spot/101189688>, accessed 21 March 2024.

43 Shells, snakes, survival: Little Congwong Beach, La Perouse

'Their ancestors continue … claim to their country': Julia Kensy,
'La Perouse', *Dictionary of Sydney*, 2008, <dictionaryofsydney.org/
entry/la_perouse>, accessed 21 March 2024.
'La Perouse is the only suburb … thousands of years': La Perouse Local
Aboriginal Land Council, 'History of La Perouse', 2023, <www.
laperouse.org.au/copy-of-our-background>, accessed 21 March 2024.
'"Reserve for the use of Aborigines" … from white Australia': Kensy,
'La Perouse'.
'one-fifth of La Perouse's population is Indigenous': Randwick City
Council, 'La Perouse – Philip Bay Ancestry', .idcommunity, <profile.
id.com.au/randwick/ancestry?WebID=150>, accessed 21 March 2024.

44 The film set: Palm Beach

'"a film made by pals in paradise"': Harry Windsor, '"Palm Beach": Film
review', *Hollywood Reporter*, 6 June 2019, <www.hollywoodreporter.
com/movies/movie-reviews/palm-beach-review-1216194/>, accessed
21 March 2024.

45 Skin: Maroubra Beach
'end of the 19th century … Indigenous population': Ford, *Sydney Beaches*,
    p. 90.
'I read a piece about the Bra Boys': Luke McIlveen, 'A beast surfaces: Battle
    of the beach', *Daily Telegraph*, 9 December 2005, p. 39.

46 We can be heroes: Obelisk Beach, Sydney Harbour National Park
An earlier version of this chapter was published as 'Swimming and paying
    tribute to heroic gay elders', SBS Voices, 5 March 2021, <www.sbs.
    com.au/voices/article/swimming-and-paying-tribute-to-heroic-gay-
    elders/lav9n6aow>.
'Garry Wotherspoon recounts … of the 20th century': Wotherspoon,
    Gay Sydney, pp. 50–51.

47 The superstar: Bondi Beach
'In the great Australian novel *The Tree of Man* … "many furtive lusts"':
    Patrick White, *The Tree of Man* (1955), Vintage, Sydney, 2009, p. 331.
'Peter Corris … crime-writing': Paul French, 'Is Sydney Australia's Capital
    of Noir?', CrimeReads, 8 June 2020, <crimereads.com/is-sydney-
    australias-capital-of-noir/>, accessed 29 May 2024.

48 Away from her: South Cronulla Rock Pool
'A 2014 Queensland study … happy memories': Christine Neville et
    al., 'Exploring the effect of aquatic exercise on behaviour and
    psychological well-being in people with moderate to severe dementia:
    A pilot study of the Watermemories Swimming Club', *Australasian
    Journal on Ageing*, vol. 33, no. 2, 2014, pp. 124–127.

49 City of joy: Bronte Baths
'In her book *Why We Swim* … flow': Bonnie Tsui, *Why We Swim*, Algonquin
    Books of Chapel Hill, Chapel Hill, NC, 2020.
'The *Oxford Companion to Emotion and the Affective Sciences* argues that … and
    thinking"': Cited in Matthew Kuan Johnson, 'Joy: A review of the
    literature and suggestions for further directions', *Journal of Positive
    Psychology*, vol. 15, no. 1, pp. 5–24.
'the "Australian Crawl" … Alick Wickham': Waverley Council, 'Bronte's
    baths: A history', 2008, <www.waverley.nsw.gov.au/__data/assets/pdf_
    file/0009/159327/Bronte_Baths_-_a_history.pdf>, accessed 21 March
    2024.

50 'The swamp': Lawson Swim Centre, Upper Blue Mountains
'The world has just recorded … era of global boiling"': United Nations,
     'Hottest July ever signals "era of global boiling has arrived"
     says UN chief', UN News, 27 July 2023, <news.un.org/en/
     story/2023/07/1139162>, accessed 21 March 2024.
'Across northern and north-west Australia … Spain and Thailand': Nick
     Evershed, Andy Ball and Adam Morton, 'How big are the fires
     burning in Australia's north? Interactive map shows they've burned
     an area larger than Spain', *The Guardian*, 18 November 2023, <www.
     theguardian.com/news/datablog/ng-interactive/2023/nov/15/
     bushfires-in-australias-north-this-year-have-burned-an-area-larger-
     than-the-size-of-spain>, accessed 21 March 2024.
'When steam-train services … nicknamed "the swamp"': Robyne Ridge,
     'Lawson Dam – from steam train water supply to swimming pool',
     Blue Mountains Gazette, 9 March 2018, <www.bluemountainsgazette.
     com.au/story/5275083/lawson-dam-from-steam-train-water-supply-
     to-swimming-pool/>, accessed 21 March 2024.

51 The underwater bushwalk: Gordons Bay
'*Losing Eden*': Lucy Jones, *Losing Eden: Why our minds need the wild*, Penguin,
     London, 2021.
'What's less known is … health benefits': Sergio Diez Alvarez, 'Health
     check: Why swimming in the sea is good for you', *The Conversation*,
     26 December 2016, <theconversation.com/health-check-why-
     swimming-in-the-sea-is-good-for-you-68583>, accessed 21 March
     2024.

ACKNOWLEDGEMENTS

This book came into being thanks to the kindness, knowledge and encouragement of many people.

Thank you, Catherine M Brennan, for giving me a copy of Jessica J Lee's *Turning*. Your gift propelled the first strokes of the book. As the chapters progressed, the scholarship of Caroline Ford's *Sydney Beaches: A history* fuelled inspiration and curiosity. I am very grateful to Clark Sheedy, Julia Baird, Jeanne Ryckmans and Sally Heath for supporting the project in its early days.

I owe a huge debt of thanks to Tim Baker, Catherine M Brennan and Dr Charmaine Buchanan for their insightful and constructive comments on early drafts. Thank you, David Thompson, for opening the door to publication with New-South. At every stage of the project, the NewSouth team have been gracious, warm and hugely professional. A big thank you to Elspeth Menzies and Sophia Oravecz for expertly guiding the project, to Rosina Di Marzo for promoting it with enthusiasm, to Mika Tabata for her evocative and whimsical cover design, and to Emma Driver for her sensitive and meticulous editing. Many thanks and much gratitude to Benjamin Law, Yves Rees and Ailsa Piper for their kind support.

Over the course of the swimming year, many people were enormously generous with their stories, expertise and hospitality. Thank you to Leissa Pitts; Robyn Burridge; Brett Leavy at Virtual Songlines; Ash Walker and the Gujaga Foundation; Dr James Worner and Dr Scott McKinnon; Nathan Merritt and Gary Farrar at the NCIE; Alvin and

Frankie Wong and Robert Loader; Robert Hardie, Ray Ziesing and the Wett Ones; Dr Janice Hinckfuss, Brenda McNamara and Rose Delacruz.

The book has been informed and enriched by the warmth, wit and wisdom of many people over many years. Thank you, Elizabeth Turai-kiss, Emily Owen, Sam Ow, Neal Fitzgerald, Lloyd Norris, Vikki Weston and Toni Payne for decades of inspiration and friendship, and thousands of conversations about travel, books, films and life. A big hug to my overseas adopted family of Lenka and Ládā Vašků, Susanne Ölke and Matthias Maus, Christina Liu, Connie Tsang, Nigel Sayer, Murtaza Ghulam, Alex Chu and David San Roman, Meurig Thomas, Norbert Killmaier, Maria Prosynska, Sabine Felber and Mathias Voigt, Germano Agli, Adrian Bliss and Bronwyn Owen.

Thank you to colleagues past and present who temper the business of the day with a sense of fun: Diana Kielar, Annie Jackson, John Sultana, Chrissie Austron, Jane Chaytor, Ross Vermeer, Jeffrey and Chonny Brown and Aviva Cheng, and my IDP colleagues.

A bouquet to my local gang of buddies and muses who make Sydney even more special: Bill Alexiou, Susan Busatto and Olivia and Madeleine Riordan, Patrick Seedsman and Paul Adabie, Terence Goodall, Sally Earle, Paula Hardin, Ben-Burt Smit and Maria Jones, Alex Allgood, Ben and Lara Parsons, Nigel Pittaway and Joe Menggolo, David Langston-Jones and David Underwood, Magdaline Shenton-Kaleido, David Laws, The Gang of Nine, John Wagner, Brett Fulton and Theo van der Heijdt, Marcus Reynolds, Tobin Bales, Ross Garland and the Saturday crew at NYS.

Family figures largely in this book and they matter greatly to me. I am lucky to have four brothers who have been lifelong partners in aquatic crime and the very best of friends: here's to you, Steve, Tim, Nick and Mike. Much gratitude and love to my wonderful and generous sisters-in-law, Anna, Julie, Maryanne and Margie; and to my dynamic and multitalented nephews and nieces Nick, Rose, Dave, Ivy, Nat, Harry and Maxine. Life is richer because of the company of Janica Nichols, Fiona and Tony McQueen, and the Orth Clan. Finally, to Wade, thank you for your constant love and support, for always listening and for sharing in this wonderful ride.